ADVANCE PRAISE FOR *DOUBLE DOUBLE*

"Cameron has long been a favorite resource in entrepreneurial circles, entrepreneurial companies, and at the Entrepreneurs' Organization. Cameron's reputation as a speaker and leader with the ability to help create dramatic change in companies came quickly. Through his sold-out presentations (starting with teaching entrepreneurs how to turn their name into a household name), his writings, and his lectures, Cameron has touched, and significantly impacted, thousands of entrepreneurs who have changed the way they brand and market their companies, jump-started their culture, and altered their growth trajectory with his friendly and astute guidance. Now they can learn from his book *Double Double*, too."

—Matthew K. Stewart, cofounder, National Services Group; cofounder, College Works Painting; former global chairman of the board, the Entrepreneurs' Organization

"There's growth . . . and then there's rapid growth. While most companies claim to want rapid growth, the truth is you have to be organized and ready for it. Nobody knows how to get you ready for this kind of rapid growth like Cameron Herold. Now, for the first time, he's sharing with everybody how he does it. What was once something his clients routinely spent lots of money and time on is now available to you for the price of a book. I have no idea why Cameron is giving away his strategy for such a meager fee, but I devoured each and every sentence in this book. You should too."

—Mitch Joel, President, Twist Image, and author of *Six Pixels of Separation*

"Cameron Herold has a huge passion and a remarkable ability to captivate any audience. He is a true showman with powerful messages that are easily understood. What you take away from his book *Double Double* you can implement!"

—John Rose, President, Nuheat; winner of Canada's 50 Best-Managed Companies for five consecutive years

"The content in *Double Double* helped us focus our sales efforts on the critical few. Within weeks we had a $200,000 order from one of these prospects. This customer will be a $1 million annual client for us. Before this order our largest single order was $15k. This was easily a million-dollar concept."

—Barrett Ersek, Holganix, Glen Mills, PA; Gazelle 20; Graduate of MIT BOG class; built and sold two companies

"You will not find a coach or speaker with more business acumen, relationship intimacy, depth of Rolodex, and overall passion to help people achieve their dreams than Cameron Herold. When I heard him speak, I made a decision that I would do whatever it took to spend a few extra moments of time with him. It was and continues to be one of the best decisions I have made in advancing the growth of our five companies."

—John Ruhlin, Ruhlin Partners, St. Louis, Missouri; #1 All Time International Distributor of Cutco Cutlery out of 1,000,000 in the company's sixty-year history

"Cameron's leadership, insight, and coaching has been instrumental to our success in launching and growing our franchise system. His expertise that he has included in his book *Double Double* has enabled us to grow from one to thirty-eight franchise locations in Canada in a little over three years and has us poised to expand just as rapidly across the United States. Cameron specifically helped us navigate the pitfalls of hyper-growth all the while showing us how to strengthen and grow our brand across the country."

—Ken Sim, Nurse Next Door, Vancouver, Canada; Gazelles 22; #1 Employer in BC (*BC Business* magazine); #35 Best Employer in Canada (*Globe and Mail*); #7 Best Mid-Size Franchise System in North America (*Franchise Business Review*); Ernst & Young Entrepreneur of the Year

"I've been fortunate to see Cameron speak on several occasions, and the provocative ideas he has in his book *Double Double* on building a world-class culture have helped us tremendously. We've incorporated several of his strategies, including recruitment, orientation, mentoring, performance management, and people-management practices."

—Martin Perelmuter, Speakers' Spotlight, Toronto, Canada
Ernst & Young Entrepreneur of the Year

"Cameron is a leading edge 'out of the box' thinker and presenter who is all about results. His thought-provoking material will leave you motivated to get things done!"

—Michael Drever, CEO & Founder, Expedia CruiseShipCenters International

"Little did I know when I sat down across the table from Cameron at a group dinner that by the end of the meal, I would have a profound new perspective of life as an entrepreneur. I've continued to learn from Cameron and have yet to find a single piece of bad advice. I'm looking forward to more in his book *Double Double*."

—Tim Storm, FatWallet.com, Rockton, IL; Entrepreneur of The Year 2010 Finalist; *Entrepreneur* magazine; Founding Member of Gazelles 22

"Thanks to Cameron's common-sense yet unorthodox guidance, my revenues have doubled from last year. The content in his book *Double Double*, on creating a world-class culture, changed how I do business—I used to think that 'culture' was just something for huge corporations, not a small business like mine. Now I'm in control and people are clamoring to work with me."

—Laura Roeder, LauraRoeder.com, Venice, CA

"When Cameron speaks people listen, he speaks with gravitas and passion—and his book *Double Double* now gives us a chance to get a 'Cameron Herold' fix wherever and whenever we choose. He operates in such a fabulous position of being able to drop inside leading entrepreneurial businesses. He gets what business is about this century—and we all want a piece of it."

"Cameron has been there, starting and growing companies. He truly understands what entrepreneurs have to deal with and how to help them move forward."

"As a 19-year-old budding entrepreneur, Cameron inspired me to stay out of the workforce and start my first business instead. He guided me through the challenges and gave me some of the best advice in my business career, and I've kept that advice with me all these years, from how to hire and fire people, to dealing with challenging customers, and to building a great culture in your company."

"We handle high-profile events like the Olympics and FIFA World Cup. The content in Cameron's book *Double Double* has helped me look at our organization in a more strategic way that makes me a better business owner—and a better person."

"Cameron's business philosophies in his book *Double Double* simply make sense. His mentorship has significantly helped me in managing a virtual team of leaders from across Canada in a fast-growing organization."

"Cameron was one of the first guys I worked with who recognized what I was truly good at in my job and cleared the way for me to flourish. He's honest, candid, and supportive."

"Cameron's book *Double Double* shows that he understands business like Neo sees the Matrix. I have watched him give several presentations over the years, attended the EO MIT Entrepreneurial Masters Program he taught at, and *every* time I am astonished by how insightful he is to the *successful* driving forces of any business."

"Cameron has an amazing ability to get people to execute their vision. I met Cameron at the MIT Entrepreneurial Masters Program and was struck by his ability to translate the complex into simple, doable tasks. I hired him as a coach for my team to learn his success strategies. Every day we implement the guidance from his book *Double Double* in some way, making our organization much more effective and efficient."

—Jason Beans, Rising Medical Solutions, Chicago, IL; Inc 5000 (2008, 2009, 2010); PCI Index (first company with six quarters straight)

"Learning from Cameron has helped me embrace the entrepreneurial roller coaster by leveraging the manic highs through energizing my people and generating PR in addition to being cautious during the lows. The concepts in his book *Double Double* shifted my viewpoint and have literally catapulted my business."

—Bryan Ravit, Founder, universiDVD, West Palm Beach, FL; Winner of *Miami Herald*'s Business Plan Challenge

"Cameron Herold has helped me in two major ways. First, he inspires you to get the most out of your team by focusing on them, not on you. Secondly, he teaches the power of public relations in simple, executable terms. Thanks for including these lessons in your book *Double Double*. Culture and PR are amazing influences on success."

—Dan Stevens, President, Workerbee TV, Winnipeg, Canada; EO Global President, 1996–1997

"Most entrepreneurs have many visions (at once) about how to grow their business. Through his speaking, DVDs, and coaching, Cameron helped my company focus all of the visions into a painted picture. And more importantly, he created a process that allowed us to prioritize and action-plan all the ideas that seemed to be floating around indefinitely. Thanks to Cameron, our company now functions more rhythmically, whereas before it was constantly in a state of mania."

—David Mammano, NextStep.com

"I have always looked to you as a mentor and am always inspired by your speeches, your style, and the way you live your life. You are probably not aware, but you have been a big part of my inspiration around chasing my dream of doing speaking events, and I thank you for that."

—David Reeve, Franchise Operations, Champion of the Dream Program, Nurse Next Door

"Cameron's DVD, *Generating Free PR*, has been instrumental in FROGBOX getting North America wide publicity. With Cameron's help we were chosen as one of *Entrepreneur* magazine's Top 10 Hot Startups for 2010 and have been written up in the *Globe and Mail*, *Costco Connection*, and countless other publications."

—Doug Burgoye, FROGBOX, Vancouver, Canada

"Over the years Cameron has given me great insight and practical advice in my professional speaking career. Not only does he have extraordinary stage presence as a presenter, he has the rare combination of being able to coach speakers as well."

—Eddie Osterland, M.S., La Jolla, CA; 1st Master Sommelier in USA

"Listening to Cameron live and later on his DVDs has made a tremendous impact on my business and management style. He simplifies management by focusing on old and proven management concepts. I make all my managers watch Cameron's videos on corporate culture."

—Dino Manosa, Manosa Properties, Manila, Philippines

"Cameron Herold offers great coaching tools to world leaders. He has inspired me and my team with great stories, insights, and tips you can put to use in your business and in your life."

—Gerardo Briones, Promogroup, Mexico City, MX

"Energy. Honesty. Vulnerability. Creativity. Experience. Boardroom savvy meets street smarts. Cameron Herold is a lifelong entrepreneur and learner. Cameron's insights in his book *Double Double* have helped me view business topics from different angles. His bold, creative ideas have inspired me to unleash the power of 'what box' thinking to meet my business goals."

—Gregory Keyes, Affant Communication, Costa Mesa, CA

"Cameron Herold, like all great thought leaders, is an enigma to me. I have never met anyone who could take something as complex as marketing and public relations for billion-dollar companies and make it seem so simple as he's done in his book *Double Double*. Every time I have the privilege of being around him I walk away feeling like I can tackle the world. Because of Cameron I am a better visionary, marketer, and CEO."

—Hunter Ingram, HometownQuotes, Franklin, TN

"I attribute a large part of our success to the insights and ideas I learned from my many conversations with Cameron over the years. His ideas around culture and PR have helped us achieve several national and local 'Best Places to Work' awards, as well as three back-to-back appearances on the INC 5000 and SBA Small Business Person of the Year for the state of Nevada. As the Learning Chair of the Las Vegas Chapter of the Entrepreneurs' Organization, I have twice flown Cameron down to speak to our local members and entrepreneurs, and he is one of our highest rated speakers."

—Jade Anderson, Capstone Risk Management & Insurance, Las Vegas

"Hearing Cameron speak has helped me tremendously as a business owner. The three takeaways from Cameron that have made the biggest impact on my business have been:

Paint the future.

Have the right people—raising the bar raises results.

Reverse engineer the future, work backward, and have a plan with metrics! Cameron's content is extremely practical, something I can digest and implement right away."

—Jasen Ko, ActMedia, Philippines

"After watching Cameron's DVDs, we immediately put a *ton* of his business practices into our daily business activities. His 'reverse engineering' approach to business, coupled with the TOP 5, has helped propel our system sales growth by an astonishing 60 percent in the first eighteen months of using it. Thanks, Cameron, your DVDs are worth their weight in gold!"

—Lane Martin, Modern Purair, Kelowna, Canada

"Cameron has a remarkable ability to understand the strategy of just about any industry. In just a few sentences of description, over the phone, he helped me completely change the way I thought about my market and target audience. He is truly gifted."

—Lester Baskin MD, Baskin Clinic, Portland, OR

"Cameron impacted more my effectiveness as a leader in a ninety-minute live speech than any other person has before. He is straightforward, transparent, and passionate about transmitting his own experience in growing companies, and fast and willing to make it happen in your company as well."

—Luis I. Cortes, Polymita, Barcelona, Spain; Top 100 Entrepreneurial
Company in Spain by *Emprendedores* magazine and Top 10
best technology companies in Europe

"Cameron's coaching and DVDs made me realize the true vision and direction for our company. He then showed us the steps on how to make that dream a reality. I especially enjoyed the secrets to unlocking tons of free PR for your business."

—Matt Shoup, M&E Painting, Loveland, CO; 2009 "40 Under 40 Award"
by the Northern Colorado Business Report; Top 25 Most Influential
Young Professionals; *Colorado Biz* magazine, 2010

"Cameron's lightning-fast delivery serves up quick hits of colorful concepts and rich inspiration for an equally speedy marketplace. He is a master at reminding us that it's not about boiling the ocean—it's about leveraging the big and small opportunities that come our way as quickly and creatively as possible."

—Peggy Smith, Worldwide ERC, Arlington, VA

"He had success operating a business. The lessons in his book *Double Double* are real and they work. I see two distinct periods in time for my company: before Cameron, and after Cameron. Before, I was just running a business that happened to make money. It was a poor business and I didn't enjoy it. After, employees started randomly coming up to me and telling me they were 'extremely happy and blessed to work here.' Awesomeness was everywhere, our hiring systems were better, our culture improved considerably, our clients were happier, and thankful testimonials started to pour in. Our revenues had also increased 106 percent year over year. Do I recommend Cameron Herold to entrepreneurs? Hell yeah."

—Richard Cooper, TotalDebtFreedom.ca, Markham, Canada; PROFIT HOT 50, 2008 & 2009; Ernst & Young nominee for Entrepreneur of the Year, 2010

"Cameron has saved my company time and money, and has added wisdom, experience, and knowledge. He provides clarity to our team and brings structure, systems, and processes that have saved years of mistakes."

—Karen Stewart, CEO, Fairway Divorce Solutions, Calgary, Alberta, Canada

"Cameron helps me confront the tougher aspects of my business. After ten years of 50 percent compounded growth, (mt) has non-trivial operational challenges. He provides the answers I need in an inspiring, contributive, and relevant way."

—Demian Selfors, CEO, (mt) Media Temple, Los Angeles

"You have changed my entrepreneurial journey for the better."

—Razor Suleman, CEO, I Love Rewards, Toronto, Canada; Top 100 Employer in Canada, 2006 & 2007

"Everyone has read the best business books, but nobody does any of the stuff. Cameron has helped me lead sustained change in my business and performance over just a few months."

—David Jaffa, Chairman, SAM Learning Ltd, London, UK

"He's provided us with the systems and the proper mind-set to scale our business by working *on* our business instead of *in* our business. It certainly feels like we're scaling—our goal is to grow by 300 percent+ this year. Cameron understands the unique challenges faced by entrepreneurs who want to grow their companies really fast. He uses surprisingly simple tools and processes that can really help you get into hyper-growth mode. Buckle up."

—Adrian Salamunovic, Cofounder, CanvasPop.com, Ottawa, Canada

"The level of depth and attention to detail he has in his business is mind-boggling. Any company would be lucky to have Cameron on their side dissecting the details and projections, and taking the 'mystery' out of why a business is growing or failing."

—Michael Schneider, CEO, MobileRoadie.com; LA *Business Journal's* Top 20 In Their 20s, 2008

"We were flying by the seat of our pants and making it up as we went. With Cameron's help we were able to create a vision, mission, and culture; focus on a clear path to the future; and create a franchise system that made sure we had the right people on the bus with us. He gave us the courage to get rid of the wrong people, and we are now doing more revenue with less franchises."

—Steve Baines, CEO, Envirofoam, Calgary, Alberta, Canada

"I have known Cameron Herold for more than twenty years, and have sought his business counsel over this time at various junctures in my business life. He has proven to not only be thorough, but also and most importantly inspirational."

—Robert Sneddon, CastleMoore

"Cameron has amassed so many great entrepreneurial experiences that it occurs to me now that I haven't described a challenging situation to him yet which he didn't have a relevant and insightful parallel experience to share. Significant ground has been covered in both my professional and personal lives, in ways that I hadn't imagined possible or necessary, since first meeting Cameron."

—Sean Costello, IronGate Server Management & Consulting, Profit Hot 50, 2008 & 2009, *Ottawa Business Journal* 40 under 40

"Cameron has really been an inspiration in helping me take my organization to the next level by investing in attitudes rather than capital. I hadn't previously realized completely how important it was to focus on office culture."

—Shami Sandhu, RE/MAX River City, Edmonton, Canada; 2010 *Avenue Magazine* Top 40 under 40

"Cameron is one of the most articulate and forward-thinking speakers I have had the pleasure to meet. The enthusiasm and interaction are quite spectacular, and every time I find myself hanging on his every word. He challenges me to broaden my horizons and inspires me to think outside of the box. I am most impressed with the actual simplicity of what he shares and left with a feeling that I too am capable of following his lead."

—Shawn Lane, Cheyenne Marketing, Las Vegas, Nevada

"I saw Cameron at an Entrepreneurs' Organization event. It definitely opened my eyes to some very creative techniques to brand your company, engage staff, and stretch a marketing budget with creative promotions. I 'invested' in his DVDs to share with my leadership team. For someone who is in the business of marketing, it was humbling to observe how creatively Cameron thinks."

—Tim Padgett, Pepper Group, Palatine, IL; back-to-back-to-back *BtoB Magazine* Top Agency Recognition, 2008-2009-2010

"Watching Cameron since childhood has been a constant learning situation and always an interesting one too! He's been ahead of his time as an entrepreneur and businessman since he was my very first boss on our paper route and then again as a teenager while he was in university and running the local College Pro Painters franchise."

—Todd Herold, President, Herold Supply, Sudbury's top 40 under 40, professional long driver (Golf)

"I was fortunate enough to have met Cameron early in his career. Even then his ideas provided the inspiration that helped me immediately launch my own business career on return to Australia. He even introduced me to my wife!"

—Warren Waddell, Pro Flooring, Sydney, Australia

"I'm a repeat entrepreneur and Cameron inspired me to start my most recent company Pixability. He's been at my side through ups and downs. We practice a lot of the ideas in his book *Double Double* in our company on a daily basis, and it's really helped our growth. Cameron's enthusiasm for growing companies is infectious—so read this and become infected with the growth virus!"

—Bettina Hein, Pixability, Cambridge, MA; SmallBiz HotTech Award

"We have experienced Cameron as an excellent trainer and teacher for our company, with visionary, creative, and unique approaches that brought lots of new insights and new successful directions and excellent results. Cameron is one of the best marketing specialists that we know of!"

—Anja Puhlmann, Kins Group, Zurich, Switzerland

"I saw Cameron in Las Vegas during the Entrepreneurs' Organization University and his story of building a fast-growth company and learning lessons helped give me insights into how to grow my company into one of the world's fastest growing companies. He is a great businessman and someone you can learn a lot from."

—Nick Kho, Real Social Dynamics, Los Angeles; INC 5000

"I have learned plenty of things from Cameron, but most all funnel in to one category and that is 'confidence.' He showed me in many ways that if I am confident in the pursuit of my goals that the chances of success will be much greater. As I look back at victories and my losses, it is proven he was right."

—Guy Rubino, Rubino Restaurants

"What I truly value when I hear Cameron present is the fact that I know I will learn something practical that I can implement right away and get an immediate ROI from. As President of a fast-growth company I need someone to bring clarity to the day-to-day issues I face. Cameron does just that."

—Stephen Kearley, Benson, Kearley IFG Insurance, Toronto, Ontario, Canada; Director, Entrepreneurs' Organization

"Cameron provided us invaluable PR information that allowed us to score a half-page article in a major newspaper. That article caught the eye of Tressa Wood, who would eventually become our CEO and help lead the Men in Kilts North American franchise launch! Now he's revealed his secrets in the book *Double Double*."

—Brent Hohlweg, Cofounder, Men in Kilts

"Cameron is a business stud. His approach to PR in particular, and business in general, is refreshing, direct, and wholesome. While there are many business gurus out there spouting their wares, Cameron has really done it, and offers useable, practical advice in his book *Double Double*."

—Mike Faith, founder of Headsets.com, an Inc. 500
and Winning Workplaces company

"Cameron has impacted me and my business more than any other speaker or consultant. The difference with Cameron is his coaching is so much more practical and applicable. We have implemented his PR tactics and have quadrupled our press/media coverage; we have implemented the dream manager program he introduced to us, resulting in an incredible culture; we have implemented his coaching on providing the right tools to our employees—leading to increased productivity, nearly zero turnover, and multiple awards. I wholeheartedly recommend Cameron's book *Double Double*."

—Clint Drawdy, Hire Methods Recruiting, Jacksonville, FL;
INC 500 (1) and INC 5000 (2)

DOUBLE
DOUBLE

How to Double
Your Revenue and
Profit in 3 Years or Less

CAMERON HEROLD

GREENLEAF
BOOK GROUP PRESS

Published by Greenleaf Book Group Press
Austin, Texas
www.gbgpress.com

Distributed by Greenleaf Book Group LLC

For ordering information or special discounts for bulk purchases, please contact Greenleaf Book Group LLC at PO Box 91869, Austin, TX 78709, 512.891.6100.

Design and composition by Greenleaf Book Group LLC and Alex Head
Cover design by Greenleaf Book Group LLC

Publisher's Cataloging-In-Publication Data
(Prepared by The Donohue Group, Inc.)

Herold, Cameron.
  Double double : how to double your revenue and profit in 3 years or less / Cameron Herold. -- 1st ed.
  p. ; cm.
  "A BackPocket COO guide."
  ISBN: 978-1-60832-099-8
  1. Industrial management—Handbooks, manuals, etc. 2. New business enterprises—Management—Handbooks, manuals, etc. 3. Entrepreneurship—Handbooks, manuals, etc. 4. Success in business. I. Title.
HD62.5 .H47 2011
658.4/21   2010939899

Part of the Tree Neutral® program, which offsets the number of trees consumed in the production and printing of this book by taking proactive steps, such as planting trees in direct proportion to the number of trees used: www.treeneutral.com

Printed in the United States of America on acid-free paper

11 12 13 14   10 9 8 7 6 5 4 3 2 1

First Edition

This book is dedicated to a few important people in my life:

To my boys, Aidan and Connor—if you choose the entrepreneurial path like your great-grandfathers, grandfathers, and father did, you'll have some of my lessons to help guide you.

To my Papup, Cas Herold—I hope you see that I've tried.

To my father, John Herold, and Grandpa, Cam Shortts—I learned so much from each of you about running a company and the value of hard work. You turned me into an entrepreneur. Thank you.

To my mother, Judy Herold—you always helped me and showed me that I could do any business I tried. And I miss you *so* much.

And finally, to my wife, Jane Sydie—it's cliché, but true: you allowed me to be an entrepreneur. You rode the roller coaster with me, at times silently wondering what was happening. You allowed me to work late nights, to work from our bedroom, and to work when the feeling grabbed me. You always told me I was smarter than I believed I was. I love you.

CONTENTS

ACKNOWLEDGMENTS

So many people have helped me learn as a leader. So many have helped me build companies. So many have given me confidence to share what I know how to do. And so many more have pushed me to write this book and helped me get it done, for, God knows, I didn't want to do it.

To sum up my thanks—to all of you—"Thank you, sincerely, for being my friend." And to those I've missed, for letting me buy you a drink later to say "Sorry."

Akash Sablok	Ben Hoskins	David Crombie
Alan Remer	Ben Houta	David Harrop
Alana Winter	Boris Wertz	David Hassell
Albert Koopman	Brad Whitmore	David Mammano
Alex Shippillo	Brian Scudamore	Dawn Mucci
Alex Wray	Brock Bulbuck	Debra Milne
Alexis Neeley	Brock Chapman	Don Darby
Allison Nazarian	Bruce Chisholm	Doug Davidoff
Alycia Edgar	Bruce Sellery	Drew Boyles
Amy Chan	Cathy Hirst	Eliot Burdett
Andrea Baxter	Chris Morgan	Eric Patel
Andrew Sherman	Chuck Hall	Evan Rudowski
Andy Levine	Clint Drawdy	Frank Stillone
Arnout Orelio	Clint Greenleaf	Gini Dietrich
Ashley Denief	Conor Neill	Gregg Johnson
Ashley Perona	Corey Bell	Greig Clark
Belinda Miller-Foey	Dan Lionello	Helen Sheridan
Ben Hopper	David Chalk	Ian Portsmouth

J Williams

Jack Daly

Jade Anderson

Jade Mulcair

Jake Boxer

James Jones

Jane Sydie

Jasen Ko

Jason Abernathy

Jason Beans

Jason Billingsley

Jeannette Montgomery

Jesse Korzan

Jillian Dixon Boxer

Jim Courtney

Jim Ward

JL Vanhulst

Joe Stellega

John DeHart

John Herold

John L. McCarty

John Rose

John Stepleton

Jonathan Kay

Josh Friedman

Joshua Burnett

Judi Richardson

Junior Gupta

Ken Bautista

Ken Sim

Kevin Carter

Kevin Geddes

Kimbal Musk

Kimberly Appleton

Kristi Herold

Laura Roeder

Laura-Lynn Tyler
   Thompson

Lee Prosenjak

Les McKeown

Lucy Cornell

Maher Daoudi

Marc Russo

Marie Wiseman Prairie

Mark Moses

Mark Rubin

Mary Mowbray

Matt Fraser

Matt Stewart

Michael Caito

Michael Jagger

Michael Romley

Michael Schneider

Michel Falcon

Michelle Rodger

Mike Drever

Mo Fathelbab

Natalie Sisson

Nik Van Haeren

Paul Guy

Paul Hayman

Peter Shankman

Praveen Kaler

Praveen Varshney

Razor Suleman

Rebecca Page

Rich Schiavo

Richard Cooper

Rick Broadhead

Rob Hunt

Rol Miller

Ron Martin

Roy Kime

Samantha Smith

Sarah Robinson

Scott Allison

Scott Bornstein

Scott Damron

Scott Homenick

Scott MacDonald

Scott Mossip

Sean Costello

Sebastien Tondeur

Shami Sandhu

Shane Gibson

Shannon Gavin

Shawn Lane

Shelly Random

Simon Sinek

Stephen Norris

Steve Rogers

Steve White

Sunny Cervantes

Susan Mealer

Terry Smith

Tim Danley

Tim Ferriss

Todd Herold

Tonia Brown

Tony Ricciardi

Tressa Ruehs

Tyler Wright

Verne Harnish

Victoria Klaussen

Yanik Silver

INTRODUCTION

Double Double.

That's right. This book will show you how to double the size of your company's revenue and profit in three years. The steps I describe to achieve 100 percent growth of your business over three years are simple, but they require one absolutely essential discipline.

Focus.

If you are an entrepreneur and the leader of a $500,000 to $50 million company, you have to focus intently on everything you do to grow quickly and successfully. There's no room for running around unsure of what you're doing and why. Everything must be on target and geared toward that specific growth goal.

The idea of doubling your business may seem intimidating, but it only requires growing your business 25 percent per year for three years. This is fast growth, but not hyperfast growth. And it's the kind of growth I've helped dozens of companies in seventeen different countries achieve.

The doubling we are talking about here includes not only doubling the revenue of your company but also doubling the amount of profit it makes, and doubling the amount of free time for you and your employees to enjoy.

My current clients range from $3 million to $240 million in gross revenues. I have a popular blog and more than seven thousand followers on Twitter. A lot of people are listening to what I have to say about growth. Some have achieved between 50 percent and 100 percent growth per year. Few individuals, however, have the determination or the stamina to maintain their focus and achieve their goals.

This book will show you how to double your company's revenue and profits through the simple, actionable steps of focused planning, focused building, and focused leadership. The hardcore business principles I provide are enhanced by the firsthand examples I occasionally share to illustrate the steps in action. I've arrived at these steps by sifting and winnowing my own considerable workplace experience. And I have further saved you time and trouble by closing the book with a chapter that gives you fifty-eight "Focus Points" you should concentrate on to stay on track to double.

If you do what I suggest in this book, you—like myself and other entrepreneurs I've coached—will double the size of your company's revenues and profits and the amount of your and your employees' free time.

So, let's take the first actionable step toward doubling the size of your company in three years: focus on planning.

PART 1

PREPARING FOR FAST GROWTH

CHAPTER 1

VISION/PAINTED PICTURE

"Whatever the mind can conceive and believe, the mind can achieve."
—Napoleon Hill

The goal of doubling your company's size in three years is easy to accept. Who wouldn't want to do that? But accepting this goal and realizing it are two different things. To achieve it, you need to prepare for fast growth. And to do that, you need to develop a detailed vision of the future.

Many people create goals for the future but don't really have a vision of what their company will look like at that point. If revenue is supposed to triple or quadruple, what will that do to the company? How many people will need to be on board? Will you still be in the same offices? Will you have more than one location? Will you be providing different services? What might some of those look like? If creating a picture of your company is worth a thousand words, creating what I call a "Painted Picture" of your company is worth big money.

Creating this Painted Picture is the first step in doubling the size of your company. It may seem like a simple task, but experiencing that vision requires something more than looking at your business numbers. Most entrepreneurs discover that it requires a set of skills that is very different from those they normally use. How to develop these skills and envision the Painted Picture is the essential lesson of this chapter.

One caveat must be taken into account before you devote time and energy to creating a vision of your company three years out. It is not enough simply to create a Painted Picture. Everyone in your organization must focus on the same Painted Picture, and that Painted Picture must be in sharp focus. If you and your employees are not all seeing the exact same vision of what your company will look and feel like three years hence, there is no chance it will ever happen the way you see it in your mind today.

LEANING OUT INTO THE FUTURE

Have you ever observed an athlete right before a competition? The next time you watch the Olympics or World Track and Field Championships, watch the high jumpers. Most of them stand very still just before they start their run up to the bar. They close their eyes and often bob their heads up and down or even throw their heads backward a bit as they focus their imaginations and see themselves running up to the bar and thrusting their bodies over it. Then they open their eyes, stare at the bar intently, and begin to recreate in reality what they just visualized. These athletes use focus and visualization to achieve their desired results, and by imagining the obstacles they might face along the way, they prepare themselves mentally and physically for the challenge.

The focus and visualization techniques used by athletes can and should be applied to business. If you and your employees aren't prepared—mentally and in all other ways—to overcome the obstacles you might face on the path to your goals, you'll struggle to achieve them.

I first learned about this visualization process at a luncheon of the Young Entrepreneurs' Organization (now called Entrepreneurs' Organization, or EO) in 1998. I started to think of this whole process as "leaning out into the future." Eight years later, I heard another Vancouver entrepreneur, David Chalk, describe visualization as "leaning out into the future," too. Obviously, it made sense to people to think about the process this way.

Over the years since that landmark luncheon, I've had the opportunity to learn more about the visualization process from an Olympic coach and sports psychologist and to fine-tune the technique. I've had enormous success using the visualization process in many business settings.

People respond to a challenge, and a Painted Picture gives them that. When employees see what the company will look like three years out, they are clearer on where they can step up and add value to growing it.

People likewise find their work rewarding when they feel they are contributing toward a common vision. The Painted Picture allows everyone in the company to feel like they are a part of a bigger plan. And they can see with the same clarity what everyone else in the company, including the CEO, is seeing. Everyone senses they are on the same page—because they are.

When you have "leaned out" and grabbed hold of a clear vision for success, you're more likely to achieve your desired goal. That's why it's essential that you focus, develop your vision, and communicate to your employees, suppliers, shareholders, and even your clients what your business is going to look like at every stage of its growth. I'm not talking about a To Do list, a five-year plan, or a vision statement. Vision statements tend to get written by getting a whole bunch of corporate people in a room pulling together the words that best describe their business. Then they create a one-sentence vision or mission statement for the company that no one cares about or reads ever again.

A Painted Picture is so much more. A Painted Picture comes about when an entrepreneur, founder, CEO—whatever you call yourself—plants one foot in the present and then leans out and places the other in the future, in the "what could be."

I find three years the best period to cover when creating a Painted Picture. This timeline is short enough to be seen as realistic and achievable, yet long enough to allow you to realize innovative and expansive ideas. As a result, employees can incorporate the blueprint into their overarching and day-to-day goals, all the while enthusiastically striving for the picture of an even more successful future you have painted for them.

At the end of the process, your Painted Picture will consist of a three- to four-page document that describes your vision for what your company will be three years out at double its present size. This may seem like an easy thing to produce, but it isn't.

HOW TO CREATE YOUR PAINTED PICTURE

The first step in creating a Painted Picture is to start thinking about certain questions. When you peer into the future, what do you see? What do you want to be there? What materializes in front of you as the *epitome* of success? Don't worry about how you're going to build it; just focus on *describing* what you see over the next three years. One helpful exercise is to imagine that you're filming every aspect of your business: your employees, customers, supplier relationships, and so on. Play the film in your mind: what do the big picture and the details look like three years out?

In order to answer these Painted Picture questions, you'll need to free your mind from the day-to-day worries of running your business and allow yourself the freedom and concentration to visualize the future, just as Olympic athletes visualize their performances.

Here are a few steps to get you started on the right path. Although you are writing just three or four pages, they are the most important three or four pages you will ever write.

Get out of your office.

When you're creating a Painted Picture for your company, you must leave your office. If you try to work anywhere in your building, whether you're sitting at your desk or at the boardroom conference table, chances are you'll get dragged back into the daily routine and won't be able to truly let your mind wander into the future. When you're working within an office, your mind will also tend to get pulled back into specific constraints, and that's the antithesis of this exercise. Forget current metrics, daily tasks and obligations, and the looming question of "how?" and simply let your mind wander.

The best way I've found to start a Painted Picture is to sit by the ocean, go into a forest, find a spot in the mountains, or even lie down in a hammock in your backyard and just start sketching and writing (which is what I did when I wrote the Painted Picture for BackPocket COO, the company I created to help entrepreneurs turn their dreams into reality).

Turn off your computer.

Don't use a computer to start drafting the Painted Picture for your company.

If you do, you'll get sucked into the vortex of daily emails and tasks. Instead, put pen to paper. There is magic in just writing it all out by hand first. I got a sketchpad with unlined paper. Initially, it was hard for me to think abstractly because I'm so left-brained. I turned the sketchpad sideways so it was in "landscape mode" and started writing down my ideas about what my business would look like three years in the future.

Think "Where"—Not "How."

Look at the road in front of you. Don't focus on *how* you'll make it happen. When I was COO of 1-800-GOT-JUNK? I was, by choice, never a participant in the process of creating the Painted Picture because I was the "how" person. In contrast, the company's founder, Brian Scudamore, was the "where" person: he could look at the road ahead and see where he wanted it to go. If I'd been involved in crafting the Painted Picture for that company, I'd have gotten in the way by constantly thinking about *how* we'd make it happen. Now I know how to get out of the way of progress and stop asking "how?" all the time.

Think outside the box.

It's a little hard for me to get creative, but it's definitely not impossible. Bottom line: if I can do it, so can you! Creating a Painted Picture requires you to get out of your comfort zone, and I encourage you to do so. To ensure you're getting creative, think about crazy stuff— maybe something too outlandish to share at a meeting or even consider seriously.

I like to use a technique called "mind-mapping," which isn't so much formal writing as it is plopping down random thoughts onto paper and fleshing them out later. Mind-mapping allows you to brainstorm without having to provide explanations of strategies for achieving the desired goal. Here's a good rule to follow to help you unleash your creativity: if what you think about during one of these sessions seems bizarre or unlikely, it is something you should definitely include in your Painted Picture.

The Painted Picture Checklist

Pretend you traveled in a time machine into the future. The date is December 31. Three years from now. You are walking around your company's offices with a clipboard in hand.

- What do you see?

- What do you hear?

- What are clients saying?

- What does the media write about you?

- What kind of comments are your employees making at the water cooler?

- What is the buzz about you in your community?

- What is your marketing like? Are you marketing your goods/ services globally now? Are you launching new online and TV ads?

- How is the company running day to day? Is it organized and running like a clock?

- What kind of stuff do you do every day? Are you focused on strategy, team building, customer relationships, etc.?

- What do the company's financials reveal?

- How are you funded now?

- How are your core values being realized among your employees?

Cover every area of your business: culture, staff, marketing, public relations, sales, IT, operations, finance, production, communication, customer service, engineering, values, employee engagement, work-life balance, etc. Cover interactions you'll be having with all stakeholders, too. Remember that you are envisioning all these aspects of your company after it has doubled in size.

Once I had put on paper all the ideas in my head, I was then able to write a three-page description of all the thoughts I had generated through mind-mapping. I organized them by such areas as marketing, finance, IT, operations, customer service, employee engagement, and so forth.

———

In summary, a Painted Picture is a written document roughly three pages in length that describes in vivid detail what a company's highest-ranking executive envisions that company will look and feel like three years out, without detailing how each part of the vision itself will get built or put in place. It describes what the future looks like, not how you'll get there. I've included my Painted Picture on page 12, and you are also welcome to read a copy of it on my website (www.BackPocketCOO.com).

BACKPOCKET COO

PAINTED PICTURE 2013

The following vision, which I call my Painted Picture, is a detailed, high-level overview of what my own business, BackPocket COO, will look like, feel like, and act like by December 31, 2013. Sharing it with you here helps it become reality; hopefully, it inspires you to create and build your vision too!

What I Do

Why I do what I do is clear: I love helping entrepreneurs turn their dreams into reality. *How* I go about doing it is also clear: I speak at high-profile conferences attended by entrepreneurs and CEOs. I am a highly sought-after speaker, by organizations like the Young Presidents' Organization and Entrepreneurs' Organization. Speakers bureaus enthusiastically book me for top clients. My coaching programs assist CEOs and their teams in growing their companies. Companies ask me to be on their boards. Companies and their employees benefit monthly from the content I share in webinars. My books, CDs, and DVDs are helping entrepreneurs make their dreams happen all over the world.

I listen to my inner voice to help me filter my decisions. I call on and trust my gut. I'm feeling jazzed about working with entrepreneurs to make their dreams happen, even as my own dreams are unfolding. I'm making it fun, and time and money are abundant. My company is growing because entrepreneurs keep telling each other about me. Companies feel compelled to hire me because *why* I'm doing what I do resonates with them.

I only work with clients that "fit" with me, and I have a Bucket List of things I'd rather do than work with clients who don't. I share my list with anyone who asks, which helps me cross off my goals.

How I Feel

I'm already successful. I feel successful every day. I don't get caught in "The Gap," because I no longer focus on the horizon—I am already there. Everything else I do and acquire and achieve is a bonus. I'm happy in the present. I'm able to spend time taking the kids to school, have time mid-day to spend with my wife, and take frequent two to three hour lunches with friends mid-week.

People keep telling me that I look so relaxed. I feel lucky to be doing what I'm doing. My days are fun-filled and relaxing, and my time is my own. I'm excited in every interaction I have with entrepreneurs. I feel appreciated by the people I work with. I comfortably accept the praise people give me, and I let it sink in. I know I make a serious difference to the success of each of my clients. I feel confident working with companies ready to go public, so I can share in their successes. I continue to view life through a pair of rose-colored glasses. I'm exactly where I'm supposed to be.

Programs

I have figured out what's working, what I'm good at, and I'm sticking with it:

Speaking: My content is about my leadership and growth expertise. My presentations are inspired by Seth Godin, with almost no words on the slides, and delivered as a conscious stream of thought. I frequently speak to Young Presidents' Organization chapters internationally, as well as conferences run by *Inc.* magazine, *Fortune*, American Express, and TED. I cap how many speaking events I do, which raises my fee.

Workshops: I regularly book half-day and full-day workshops with companies around the world while I'm in their cities at speaking events. I also run one- and two-day Growth Camps in Vancouver and Whistler that attract companies and employees from all over North America.

DVDs, CDs, and Books: Attendees at speaking events regularly purchase my DVDs, CDs, and books for their employees, because they know it's easier than trying to reteach what they just learned.

CONTINUES

Webinars: My webinars have hundreds of subscriber companies and thousands of subscriber employees.

Coaching/Mentoring: My coaching clients stay with me for an average of twelve months. Those who leave do so because they no longer need me to guide them or to hold them accountable to their goals. I never coach more than twelve clients in any one month. My fees get raised each year for new clients, while rates for existing clients are grandfathered in.

Startup Mentoring: My program for startups attracts five new clients per year. Clients pay fees and equity to have me participate in their growth; this way, they can also benefit from my continued advice and have my name on their board. I am a sought-after mentor and coach to companies that have been funded by venture capitalists and angel investors. It has become a no-brainer for them to have me on their teams.

Boards of Directors: I am regularly asked to sit as a board director for public companies.

Culture and Spirit

My work with CEOs is a relaxing balance of rigorous work, extrasensory overload, excitement, and play. I only work with companies with whom I want my name attached. I don't compromise.

Brand/Image

My brand resonates with people. When they meet me, they "get it." I am well liked and respected. People are overheard saying, "I need a Cameron Herold." My look has a casual, confident, Robert Graham feel to it. People who know me say, "Wow, this is such a great fit for you!" My web presence and marketing material reflect all this.

Sponsors

My work attracts high-end, reputable sponsors who advertise on my laptop and iPhone. Sponsors also provide me with clothing, technology, luggage, and car leases to get their brands in front of my clients.

Leadership

Clients say that I hold them accountable for doing the things they need to do to grow their companies. Clients,I coach love setting their goals with me, as it helps drive their companies' productivity. Companies value having me on their teams as a senior leader who they normally couldn't afford. Clients consistently say that my leadership has saved them—or made them—millions of dollars.

Communication

I don't have a filter—and I'm admired for that. (I have learned, however, to stop swearing on stage.) People trust me because I say what's on my mind. I think out loud—and am respected for that. People say I'm a breath of fresh air. I don't sugarcoat things. I say what other people are thinking.

Customer Service

My clients say that I deliver everything I promised them. My client companies feel lucky to have me helping them. They feel like they have paid handsomely for my services but received great value in return. They feel like they get great value from every interaction with me. They say that I have the safety of a Volvo, the agility of a BMW, and the sleekness of an Aston Martin. They wish they had me full-time, but are thrilled to have me for the time they do.

Systems

I outsource work to virtual assistants in places like India and the Philippines, where I get quality work done at a fraction of the cost. I have learned how to build my company with no full-time employees on the payroll, but with several people who work full-time on commission. I've worked hard at systemizing everything I do in my business.

CONTINUES

Media

The media regularly turn to me as an expert. Media outlets cover what I do, and I'm frequently asked to be a regular columnist in newspapers, magazines, and blogs. This media coverage is shown on my website, which in turn builds credibility with clients and builds my personal brand.

Profitability

I continue to make a lot of money doing what I do. I have equity and stock options in many of my clients' companies, allowing me to benefit from the upside I have helped create. I am semi-retired and continue to look for ways to grow my revenues while continually working less. I am on track to have enough passive income streams and savings by age fifty that I can begin working more on social entrepreneurship. One client was so thrilled with the results they got from my services that they bought me an Aston Martin to say thanks.

Fitness

Fitness is key. I filter the clients I work with by selecting ones whose CEOs are active in sports and pursue passionate life goals outside of work. I work out or play with them while traveling to speaking and mentoring engagements. All Growth Camps include periods of active rest.

Balance

I add extra days to international trips so that I get to enjoy the country. My wife and/or kids come with me on at least two trips per year. I've begun to take the family on one global trip per year. My annual ratio of dollars earned per hotel-room night continues to increase. I still take most Fridays off. I arrange tweetups while on the road at speaking events so I don't have to eat alone. My fun factor in traveling has increased. I do at least one active event on each trip.

Mentors

I connect to those who have already "figured it out." I do what they do, so I don't have to figure it all out myself. I'm known as a "connector" because of how many people I know and regularly call on, leveraging social networks like LinkedIn, Twitter, Facebook, and A Small World.

Family and Friends

I regularly spend time with friends and family before I think of working. I only go on the road to be in cities I want to go to, or to cities where I can take family or friends with me. I turn down events that take up too much time or that have only limited benefit. My family takes what others think of as long chunks of holiday time together each year. I work on building relationships with my friends old and new, and I proactively pick up the phone to call them just to say hi. Fitness is still a very big part of my life. Each week, I spend time running, golfing, playing tennis, skiing, and working out with a personal trainer. I go hiking every summer. Burning Man is still a yearly pilgrimage. I spend time with people who are positive. I include my family and friends in my Bucket List, and try to be a part of theirs.

THE PAINTED PICTURE IN ACTION

At 1-800-GOT-JUNK? we did a great job of making the Painted Picture come to life within the offices. As I mentioned previously, Brian Scudamore was the visionary who would write down what he saw in the company's future. He handed me the first Painted Picture in October 2000, after he had spent some time sitting on his parents' dock at Bowen Island, just outside of Vancouver. It was a vision of what the company would look and feel like by the end of 2003. He didn't know *how* he'd build what he had seen that day overlooking Horseshoe Bay, but he wrote down everything that came to mind as he contemplated what the future would be like.

I've learned that implementing (much less actually creating) a Painted Picture is far from intuitive for everyone else. Most people don't think about the steps that lead to personal or business success, and those who do can become easily frustrated with the implementation process. I use the phrase "conceive, believe, and achieve" to remind myself—and others—to keep this process in perspective as they work to make the Painted Picture a reality.

"Conceive, believe, and achieve" became our mantra as we introduced the Painted Picture to everyone inside the company, with surprising results. By getting everyone to see the same big picture of the company's future, you make them your allies in helping it come true. When your Painted Picture has been given out to all your employees, an incredible alignment takes place, and they end up being as aligned as a team of fighter-jet pilots. They instinctively make decisions that are aligned with the same vision that everyone sees. It's powerful stuff.

We also introduced people outside of the company to the Painted Picture, with equally surprising results. Are you afraid someone will steal your ideas if you share them with too many people? Forget it. The reason you should put them all in writing and then give them away is that your Painted Picture doesn't show *how* you're going to do it. You're not giving away your secret sauce. What you're giving away is what the future looks and feels like for your company, and then everyone, whether they are part of the company or not, works to help you make it come true.

I have a copy of my Painted Picture for BackPocket COO on my website, I just shared it in this book, and I give it to anyone who asks about it.

I don't care if competitors see it. I want the *whole world* to see it. The more people who know with clarity what my company looks and feels like, the better chance there is that people will be able to help me make it happen. (Please share my Painted Picture with your friends for me, too.)

THE "CAN YOU IMAGINE?" WALL

In later versions of Brian's Painted Pictures, he began asking employees and Franchise Partners what they saw in 1-800-GOT-JUNK?'s future. It was pretty much like a suggestion box—employees would randomly come up with cool stuff, usually in casual discussions. They'd say things like, "Wouldn't it be cool if xyz happened in the future?"

Some of their ideas got baked into the Painted Pictures created for 2006 and again in 2009. Many of their visions were placed in large vinyl letters on what we called our "Can You Imagine?" wall. We included brief descriptions of our ideas for the future, too. Employees would share the little things they saw happening, and leadership would sign off on them before putting them up on the wall. We wouldn't know how to achieve them yet, but often we could see them happening too. The wall was less concrete than our Painted Picture—it was meant to keep people excited and dreaming about cool things the company could do. Our guests also saw it, and they often got excited too.

At 1-800-GOT-JUNK? we called our office the "Junktion," and one employee, Katie Dunsworth, envisioned it becoming a famous tourist destination (I'll go into the details in just a little while). Then there was Lindsay Peroff's vision of seeing our company on Dr. Phil, which she later made a reality.

One day when we were adding to the Can You Imagine? wall, I tossed out the idea of Harvard Business School doing a case study on us. I offered it up almost as a joke, but I really could see Harvard MBA students wanting to study 1-800-GOT-JUNK? because we were building a world-class brand.

When Harvard did finally learn about us, it wasn't by accident; it was because of our wall. You see, so many clients, vendors, and guests had seen our wall—on which our desire to be included in a Harvard case study was mentioned—that eventually someone visiting 1-800-GOT-JUNK? said,

"Hey, I know someone at Harvard who approves the cases; would you like an introduction?" Naturally, we said yes. If we'd never committed to the idea by writing it on the wall, it may never have happened, or perhaps it wouldn't have happened as easily. Either way, what we conceived and believed—getting into a Harvard case study—was actually achieved.

Another example of our mantra in action began one day when one of our marketing managers, Andrea Baxter, came up to a group of us and said, "Can you imagine our company name on Starbucks cups?" I must admit, I thought she was a bit nuts for suggesting such an idea, but I didn't say anything. When she continued, "Don't worry about *how*—it'll happen. As long as you can see it three years from now, I'll make it happen!" Then I really *knew* she was nuts, but I loved her passion and conviction.

So, when a few months later she told us the name 1-800-GOT-JUNK?, along with a related quotation, would soon be on ten million Starbucks cups across North America—for *free*—I knew once again that our mantra, "conceive, believe, and achieve," worked—and in more ways than one. Starbucks had originally told Andrea that she could put a note from our founder on the cups but *not* the company name. In response, Andrea told Starbucks: "No, you *have* to put the company name on the cup! That's part of our vision. It says so on our wall!" She sent Starbucks a picture of our Can You Imagine? wall and convinced them to include the company name. Her belief in the idea helped us achieve our goal of getting 1-800-GOT-JUNK? on ten million cups of Starbucks beverages. It was great advertising for the brand, it cost us nothing, and it also helped create more buzz about us as an awesome company to work for in Vancouver.

When Katie Dunsworth came up with the idea of our office becoming a famous tourist destination, we thought she was crazy, too. However, six years later, we were offering tours at the office every Friday, with twenty-five to thirty businesspeople in attendance. Katie's "dream" had become a reality. It's not quite a "famous tourist destination" yet, but if visitors keep telling other people and the company keeps telling the media, soon the Junktion will be a premiere office-tour destination.

So, to make the best use of your Painted Picture, take the following actions (some of which I have covered already in the examples you've just read).

Enlist support.

When you finish your Painted Picture, share it with your employees, suppliers, bankers, and lawyers. You'll then start to see people align with your goals, and the picture will become a reality.

It's incredibly beneficial for your employees, who will use your Painted Picture as a means to understand their role in the grand scheme of things. I've even seen business areas within a company form their own version of a Painted Picture that then dovetails with the overarching one. Overall, sharing your Painted Picture with in-house people will prompt them to make decisions subconsciously that are in alignment with your blueprint. Then others outside the company with whom you share your Painted Picture will also *consciously* help you make it happen because they see the employees are energized by the clarity of it as well.

Stick to a three-year Painted Picture.

The main reason to stick to the three-year timeline is that longer periods tend to overwhelm. Think of it this way: in order to create a Painted Picture, you need to keep one foot firmly planted in the present, while the other reaches out and taps tentatively on the soil of the future. If you go much further than three years into the future, you lose your balance and fall over. So, stay about three years out and write down what you see. Six months before the end of the three-year period, start crafting your next Painted Picture.

Refer often to your Painted Picture.

Over time, your company's decision making will start aligning with your Painted Picture. I suggest having all of your employees and suppliers reread the Painted Picture throughout the year. A perfect time to do this is right at the start of your quarterly planning retreat. (I'll discuss focused quarterly planning retreats in more detail in chapter 6.) At these retreats, I've found it helpful to have each person read the Painted Picture quietly and circle the key words or sentences that resonate with them. Then, go around the room and have each person read out the areas they circled. This exercise provides alignment for the whole team before the brainstorming process takes place, and it is a useful tool to assist you in planning and prioritizing future projects. At MCI, a Geneva-based global association, communications, and event-management partner, whose Painted Picture is shared below, employees actually read one section of the company's Painted Picture prior to the start of every meeting at which more than two people are in attendance. They are maniacal about staying focused on their vision so that all decisions and discussions are aligned with it.

PAINTED PICTURE HALL OF FAME

Based on my positive experiences at 1-800-GOT-JUNK?, I have introduced many organizations to the Painted Picture concept. All of the Painted Picture Hall of Famers I describe in this section did exactly what you're supposed to do with the exercise: they pushed beyond the corporate-speak and confining metrics to answer the simple question, "What's really possible for our company?" This is how you should approach the Painted Picture. Look at it as the ultimate opportunity to make your business a success.

Some of the companies I have coached have done a particularly amazing job. Here are just a few stellar examples to inspire your own creativity. (Send me an email at Cameron@BackPocketCOO.com and I'll send you a copy of these Painted Pictures and others that companies around the world have written.)

RedBalloon

RedBalloon, the leading web provider of gift experiences throughout Australia and New Zealand, did a great job with their Painted Picture. They made it jump off the page by having a designer use creative typography—cool fonts, animation, colors, and varied type sizes—to keep the reader engaged and excited.

Nurse Next Door

Nurse Next Door, a provider of elderly home health care services in the United States and Canada, brought their Painted Picture to life brilliantly by creating a simple PowerPoint slideshow accompanied by an audio recording, in which cofounder Ken Sim reads the document as it is highlighted with photos and graphics on the slideshow. The visuals are an excellent feature that gets the reader engaged and anchors the ideas. I loved when they shared their Painted Picture on YouTube. (My only issue with theirs is that they leaned too far out—in some parts ten to twenty years.)

MCI

The CEO of MCI, a global association, communications, and event-management partner, filmed a fantastic introduction to his company's Painted Picture. What you see is Sebastien Tondeur standing in front of a screen on which the company graphics appear as he explains what the MCI Painted Picture is and why he has written it. Go to http://snipurl.com/5t7g3 for an entertaining look.

Sebastien's company was operating in twenty-five countries when I first helped him write the Painted Picture. Afterward, he brought me to a company meeting to speak with the leaders of each country's division so I could explain the idea behind the concept of a Painted Picture to them. It was a great way to introduce the idea and instantly start to trickle MCI's Painted Picture down to all eight hundred employees.

—

What I have witnessed firsthand in the workplace is that the visualization techniques taught by Olympic coaches are as applicable to the business world as they are to high-performance athletes. In creating a Painted Picture, you shouldn't worry about *how*; instead, focus on the end result, the vision of success. By involving employees in implementing your Painted Picture, you'll essentially be enlisting people to help make that vision of success a reality.

While your mind is racing with ideas, why not start writing them down right now? Start jotting down the initial ideas you have for your company. What's it look like three years from now?

Once you've committed to sketching your vision for the future, to painting your picture, you'll be well equipped to "reverse engineer" your own success.

CHAPTER 2

REVERSE ENGINEERING YOUR GOALS AND PROJECTS

"If you don't know where you're going, any road will get you there."
—Adapted from Lewis Carroll's
Alice's Adventures in Wonderland

In order to make your Painted Picture a reality, you have to take action. And in order to take action, you have to focus on setting goals for that action. It's curious, but instead of focusing on the future as you set goals and create an action plan, you have to work backward. Yes, *backward*. What that means is that you have to first identify and articulate your goals, and then find the means to achieve those objectives. You are, in effect, "reverse engineering" your successful business.

The practice of reverse engineering dreams and plans for the future was something we introduced at my first real company, College Pro Painters, back in 1986. At the time of its inception, we called it a "work-back plan." We used our work-back plan after identifying all of our goals as a company and a team.

When I was twenty-one and running College Pro Painters, I used metrics daily, but at the time I didn't know how critical they were. I actually reverse engineered the entire company to give me the profit I wanted, and I tracked it daily for each job. I knew I wanted to make $12,000 profit that first summer, and to do that, I worked out all the numbers to figure out how it would be possible. I determined the revenues I'd need to give me the net profit I wanted. I figured out the gross margin I had to earn to cover the overhead and leave me with that identified profit. I knew the number of jobs I'd need, how many painters would have to be working, and even the exact gross margin per labor hour that we'd need in order to achieve our goals. From all of those numbers, I created daily, weekly, and monthly targets. Then I measured everything and worked like a monomaniac to make them all happen. And they did.

If you wanted to reverse engineer double-digit growth, that's easy too. In fact, we did it at 1-800-GOT-JUNK? when we decided in a projection that we'd take our sales from $2 million to $100 million in five years. We simply built a spreadsheet working the number from year five back to year one. We looked at different scenarios and picked assumptions that we liked and felt we could control. We figured out what the revenues had to be each year. We figured out where those sales would come from, who we'd need in place to make it happen, and so forth. In fact, we even had org charts drawn for the upcoming three years so we could get a better visual on what the company looked like three years out, two years out, etc. We built a detailed spreadsheet showing as many areas of the company's numbers we could imagine and define. Then we described in as much detail what each year going forward would look like.

Instead of flying by the seat of their pants, entrepreneurs can use reverse engineering to align all of their daily tasks and operations with overarching objectives. I wouldn't try to get too detailed in reverse engineering anything more than one year out, though, as too many variables can change.

To put it in more general terms, reverse engineering your company is a lot like building a custom home. In this scenario, the finished product— the home—is the equivalent of our Painted Picture. But before creating it, homebuilders meet with clients and ask them to describe all kinds of areas of the home they want built or renovated. They get photos from clients, and then they draft sketches based on these photos and other information. After a few discussions to determine precisely what the clients want, the desired home begins to take shape in the clients' and homebuilders' minds. The plans the builder and architect then draw up show a clear Painted Picture of what the home should look like.

Using the plans as a guide, construction workers, electricians, plumbers, and other team members build—or reverse engineer—the client's dream home. Custom home construction is the perfect example of reverse engineering in action: by starting with what the home should look like, all of the players on the team, from construction workers to the folks putting the paint on the walls, know exactly what they're supposed to do. Everyone's role is clear and the desired outcome is too. It should work the same way in your organization, and it *can*—but only if you use a Painted Picture as a guide.

START WITH YOUR CURRENT STRENGTHS AND WEAKNESSES

Before you start putting the plans for your company into action, you have to have a clear idea of your starting point. Where you *are* with your business and where you *want to be* are two entirely different things for most organizations. One of the best tools for getting started in the process of reverse engineering your Painted Picture is to begin with an inventory of your company or business areas as they stand today. Don't be put off by the arduous process of identifying strengths and weaknesses; most of the executives I've worked with struggle with this evaluation. It's not easy, but one of my favorite ways to determine the current state of your business is through a SWOT analysis. And it needn't be arduous at all. I've helped some companies do theirs in thirty minutes.

SWOT stands for "Strengths, Weaknesses, Opportunities, and Threats." Sitting down to analyze each of these terms as it relates to your company can be extremely eye-opening. Give all of the key people in your company or leadership team a stack of Post-it notes (or any small pieces of paper). Give them ten minutes at most to write down one idea per note pertaining to the four areas represented in the SWOT. When time is up, have each person read each of his/her notes out loud and post them up on a wall according to the four categories. After everyone does this, start taking stock of the current state of your company, and then compare that with where you want to be in the future. This will give shape to the key projects you need to complete in order to make the future happen the way you want it to. Those projects will serve as the starting point for your own process of reverse engineering.

ESTABLISH SMART GOALS

Once you have an idea of the key projects you wish to undertake, you have to establish goals for each of those projects. Remember, your Painted Picture is your ultimate objective. However, to keep projects and tasks in check and in alignment with the Painted Picture, you need to streamline the list of projects by making sure that the goals for each one are SMART. I use these guidelines to help me evaluate each goal (mine feature a slight variation on the popular business acronym):

S = Shared—Sharing goals with a coach, mentor, or team member adds a little extra pressure to hit them. I even share them with suppliers and clients.

M = Measurable—Put a number on each goal so you can easily see whether the goals were hit or missed. Make the goals clear; hazy goals produce hazy results.

A = Attainable—Your goal has to be at least remotely possible for it to be included.

R = Relevant—Ensure that all goals are worth working on.

T = Time-based—Put a specific date on goals if they're due before the end of the quarter or fiscal year. For example, why not set December 12 as a deadline rather than December 31?

Every company will have projects related to these four fairly standard goals:

Revenue—Determine a solid revenue goal for the next twelve months. This is easy. Your goal should be a yearly 25 percent increase for the next three years.

Profit—Employees need a profit goal to guide them. So, to grow successfully, your company needs to tell the employees how much money the company needs to make. That way they are clear on what decisions they need to make.

Customer Service—Tie this to a measureable outcome. For instance, what is the Net Promoter Score (the percentage of your company's promoters versus its detractors) among customers going to be—40 percent, 50 percent, 60 percent?

Employee Satisfaction—Again, tie this to a measurable outcome. For instance, what is the Net Promoter Score going to be among employees—40 percent, 50 percent, 60 percent?

As you establish SMART goals for these four areas, you should also consider goals for the various other categories in your Painted Picture. The company needs a total of four to five main goals. Once these goals are picked, you can break them down into sub-goals for other business areas, people, etc. Those same goals determine which projects need to happen first.

High-performing people set goals religiously and track them religiously. They obsess about whether they're hitting or missing those goals, and why. If you don't set and track goals, life just passes you by. Make sure that you hire people who already set goals in their personal and business lives, and it won't be such a stretch to have them setting clear goals in the business each quarter, month, and week. It's just as critical to hire people with a track record of hitting their goals.

SMART PERSONAL GOALS

Life isn't just about goals for your business, though. My goals also include the amount of free time I want in my personal life. I set goals for the amount of "free days" I'll have. A free day for me is a twenty-four hour period with no email, no business journals, no business magazines, no newspapers, and not a single phone call. It's twenty-four hours of free time to spend time on the fun stuff in life with the people I love.

In 2009, my goal was to have 120 free days. In the end, I had more than 150, although I got a bit sloppy and checked email randomly from my darn iPhone. I took close to ninety Saturdays and Sundays off, not working at all. I also took twenty-one perfect consecutive free days at our cottage in the summer and left my iPhone and laptop in Vancouver. I'm doing it again this year for sure.

Having the discipline to take these days off is the kind of focus you need in order to give yourself real work-life balance. Like your business goals, your personal goals should also be SMART.

SET YOUR BOUNDARIES

Once you have the goals set and the team is committed to hitting them, the next thing you need to do is discuss boundaries. That is to say, *yes*, you want to hit these goals, but at what expense? Would you work ninety hours a week to hit them or, at maximum, forty-five? Would you give up equity in the company to raise money to help you hire people to hit the goals? What *won't* you do? Are the things you are committing to do within your company's core values?

Here are some topics that are worth discussing while you create your own list of boundaries.

- Amount of debt you'll take on
- Number of hours you'll work
- Number of days you're willing to travel
- Percentage of profits you will share, 0–100 percent
- Percentage of equity you will give up in the company, 0–100 percent
- Number of acquisitions you will make, if any
- Willingness to fire "C" or "B" players

It's critical to have the discussions in advance. Boundaries are like values: you can't compromise them to win.

FROM GOAL SETTING TO TASK IDENTIFICATION

Once you've done your SWOT analysis and clearly know your current state, identified your key projects, and set your goals and boundaries, it's time to create an action plan.

After all, what's the good of having a goal without having a plan for the steps you'll need to take to reach it? Once goals are established, I like ensuring that a step-by-step action plan is in place for each goal. Too often people set great goals but they don't take five minutes to think about what tasks need to happen to hit each goal.

Make sure that the action plan you outline for each goal answers each of the following questions.

- What precisely has to happen?
- In what order will the steps be taken?
- Who will complete each step?
- When will each step be done?
- What is the cost?
- What other business areas are involved (and do they know you need them)?
- Will a check-in with a supervisor or subordinate be needed?

I compare this to planning a dinner party. Think about all the little things that have to happen when you are the host: inviting guests, determining the seating arrangement, finding out in advance if anyone has food allergies, planning the menu, chopping the ingredients, preparing the recipes, setting the table, and, finally, serving the wine and the sumptuous meal. All of these tasks do not happen simultaneously, of course. It takes planning in order to figure out which are the high-priority tasks that need to be done first so others can be completed later.

Put the action steps in chronological sequence so that you can see the logical work-back plan, the reverse engineering. Remember, you need to start with a vision in mind and then work backward to make the vision a reality.

CHOOSING KEY PROJECTS

Now the fun begins! You're going to outline all of the projects that will make your Painted Picture a reality. Now, before you get started, keep this in mind: while this list is exhaustive, your resources probably aren't. This list will serve as a starting point from which you'll determine the critical projects to undertake, and in what order they should be taken, to move the company forward in making the Painted Picture a reality.

Before committing to a project to meet a goal, make sure you spend time thinking about what the potential return on investment (ROI) is going to be in terms of time, money, and/or resources. Is each project really worth it? Even the act of regularly setting goals is critical to driving hard and pushing to get more of the right projects and tasks completed; otherwise, people tend to get diverted by busy work or get caught up in email.

It's often not about picking which projects to do but rather which projects *not* to do that will set you up for success. Recently I had a debate with a woman on Twitter. She was telling people to spend one hour a day on promoting their company on Twitter. I said, "Really? Do you really want people spending one out of eight hours every day Tweeting? Why? What's the ROI they are looking for from it?"

If you were going to spend 12.5 percent of your time on one activity, such as using Twitter, then you'd damn well better have a goal or ROI in mind before starting out. Do the math:

- 15 hours (3 staff members for 1 hour/day for 5 days) spent on social media/week
- $30/hour paid to people working on social media
- $450 = the cost of working on social media
- Take the dollars spent and divide by your gross margin percentage: $450 divided by 35 percent.
- $1,286 at a minimum is what you need to generate in new revenues just to pay for their time, let alone make any money from it.

This calculation is critical to make as you decide which projects will help you best achieve your goals.

Give the team input into which projects are chosen.

With this project-evaluation method in mind, it is likewise critical that you involve your leadership team. A great way to involve the team in coming up with a list of potential projects for the year or quarter is through an exercise I learned at General Electric called WorkOut. Have them put together a list of all the projects you could complete as a company in the upcoming year. I love using the Post-it note exercise again for this. It draws out a long list of all the potential things you could do, and it gives everyone a chance to be heard. Categorize all the projects that you touch on by business area (sales, marketing, and so on).

Once you have all the projects categorized, it's time to vote. Count the number of projects in each area and divide by the number of people on your team. Round that number up to get the number of votes each person will have. For example, if there are twenty-two projects listed in marketing and six people on the leadership team, each person gets four votes.

Next, have each person come up and vote on the projects they think will have the most impact on attaining the overall objective and are the most urgent in terms of the annual goals you've outlined. The leaders can distribute their four votes however they wish: four projects, one vote each; two projects, two votes each; one project with four votes; and so on.

Once that's done, tally up the votes on each project. Throw out any projects that don't get any votes. Rank the remaining projects for each category based on ROI: return on time; return on money; return on resources. I usually try to limit the projects committed to annually to two to three per area, and fifteen to twenty for the whole company.

Remember: focus on the "critical few" versus the "important many."

Map the key projects.

Once the most critical projects are identified, place them into a simple spreadsheet with these columns for each project:

- Project name
- Project number
- Goal supported
- Number of votes (Note: This helps to get rid of a few more when you see how overwhelming it looks to get a few done in one year.)

- Quarter start date
- Month project ends
- Cost/savings (Note: This does *not* include current staff salaries.)
- Days until completion
- Business areas (one column for each; e.g., IT, finance, sales, and so on, to be marked with a X that shows which areas will be impacted by the project)
- Areas that will have to be built or implemented

Once this task is completed, everyone on the team should have an overall view that will allow them to remove—in conjunction with other members of the leadership team—a few more projects that looked important but can wait a year in the overall scheme.

MILESTONES

Each project in your strategic plan can be broken down into a number of tasks. Even a project that seems relatively simple on the surface, such as "Hire a VP of sales," can require the completion of as many as fifteen smaller tasks in order to ensure the project's success. Each of those tasks will end up having a due date assigned to it. When you review all of the tasks, sorted by date, you can see the milestones for the project. Each task's date effectively becomes a milestone to show whether the project is on course to be completed on time. The person who owns the project is responsible for ensuring that all these milestones are thought out, assigned, and supported to make sure the project gets done. When leadership is certain that all the tasks have been defined and that each task is assigned to someone specifically, they can then use "situational leadership," which I'll discuss shortly, to help the team become successful.

Each project's action plan can be budgeted, measured for progress, and supported with skill development along the way. This level of detail will also allow teams and companies to execute much faster and leaner since everyone is clear about what needs to be done, by whom, and by when.

LEADERSHIP'S ROLE

The role of leadership is to align, support, and enable teams to do the work they were hired to do. Leadership's role is *not* to follow up or "hold people accountable." When the right people are hired and the right plans are in place, employees can execute the action plans effectively and leadership can support them without excessive follow-up.

Leaders focus on ensuring that people are working on projects and tasks that are aligned with the Painted Picture for the company. They ensure that team members have the commitment or emotional support to do their part in the process. Leadership can assess well in advance whether skill development is necessary on any of the individual tasks in any of the projects, because they know what everyone is working on. In addition, leadership can ensure that the proper bandwidth and resources—money, people, time, supplies, and more—are available to complete the outlined projects.

At 1-800-GOT-JUNK? we circulated a document each quarter that outlined the top three things each business area and each person was going to do in the quarter. That way, every person in the company saw what everyone else was committed to during the year. It was an easy way for us to see if we were out of alignment anywhere, long before any little hiccups became big problems.

In every company, a couple of business areas always seem to be backlogged. IT and marketing, for instance, perpetually seem to get slammed with project work that no one told them was coming or that wasn't planned with the right amount of employee hours allotted. Often what ends up happening to IT and marketing teams is that the work they have in progress falls behind as new, poorly communicated demands arise. All too often a VP of sales will say, "Hey, let's get marketing to make this look prettier, and let's get IT to tie it into the website." Tasks like these build up over time, and seemingly more for marketing and IT than for any other business area. You want to avoid this at all costs.

Once you have created your Painted Picture and reverse engineered your company, you have to focus on the most important plan of all: the path to creating a culture that is ready for fast growth.

CHAPTER 3

CREATING A WORLD-CLASS CULTURE

"Building a great company means creating something that is slightly more than a business and slightly less than a religion."
—Greig Clark, founder, College Pro Painters

Building a world-class workplace culture isn't accidental; a company has to make a conscious decision to focus on developing a plan to foster and grow a fantastic working environment for its employees. Once a company decides to actively design and build its own signature culture, the process required to grow it is sort of like chasing the horizon: you never quite get there since it's always moving, but the journey is wonderful because you see new parts of your culture unfolding along the way as your company keeps getting better.

If you want to double the size of your company in three years, building a world-class culture is key. Without a strong culture, there will be no foundation for your company's rapid growth. By focusing on culture, you will improve all aspects of your business, from productivity and hiring to customer relations and employee satisfaction. Culture is tied to all of your goals and projects. It is the background of your Painted Picture.

A good culture helps you make your company a people magnet and thus attract great employees. But, more than that, it provides employees with an environment in which they are encouraged to perform at their best level. A positive culture provides an atmosphere that allows both you and the employee to get the most out of his or her skills and creativity. Effort put into culture is not a zero-sum game: the resources you invest and the benefits you give to employees should be enjoyed by the employees, but they are also more than paid back to you. Time and effort in culture are an investment in your people and in the company as a whole.

In every industry, there are companies with fantastic cultures and others with terrible ones: Google gets it, Microsoft never has. Both have about the same amount of money and both do roughly the same thing. However, Google decided they wanted their culture to differentiate them from the Microsofts of the world, and they succeeded.

When you walk through Google's headquarters, you are immediately aware of the open space and whiteboards everywhere, placed so people can put up ideas when the spirit moves them and engage in unstructured discussion time. As you walk through Microsoft's main campus, on the other hand, you can actually *feel* a cultural void. Everyone at Microsoft sits in the dark in their private offices, cranking out code without anyone around them, without any opportunity to engage in simple human interaction.

Google has worked so hard on defining its corporate culture that others have begun to hold them to it. Google's corporate motto, "Don't be evil," is constantly mentioned in the media, while Microsoft is often portrayed as the big, bad brother in the software world.

As one of my first mentors, Greig Clark, the founder of College Pro Painters, put it: "Building a great company means creating something that is slightly more than a business and slightly less than a religion. It has to be in that zone of cult. Cult-ure."

What Greig was saying is that culture has to be more than a passing trend or some ideal to which you pay lip service. As with any aspect of culture outside of the workplace, it has to be lived, experienced, and grown in order to be sustainable.

Your Painted Picture should include all aspects of the type of culture you're interested in building so that you continue to attract people who fit with it and repel those who don't. The following section will provide pointers on how to reimagine the workplace in order to engineer the kind of culture that makes your company a people magnet.

WORLD-CLASS WORK SPACE: CREATING THE PHYSICAL ENVIRONMENT

The most important aspect of your culture is the physical environment you create. It may seem simplistic to believe that the physical space employees occupy contributes to something intangible like culture, but *work space* and *culture* go hand in hand. In many ways, your work space defines your culture.

Building a world-class culture starts at your office's front door. Great employees won't come to work in a crummy office. Work hard to create a place people want to visit each day and you'll get a head start in creating world-class culture.

Here's what you need to get started.

Clean up your act.

What does your office environment look like when you first walk in? Is it organized? Fun? Stimulating? People should be able to get an idea of what it's like to work in your office from the moment they walk through the front door.

I've mentored a company called Nurse Next Door for years now. The very first time I visited their office in British Columbia, stacks of paper and boxes were everywhere. It was a disaster, and I told them that had to change if they wanted to start attracting and retaining great employees. They listened, and every week since they have held "Wasteless Wednesday," a day when they throw out anything they can to make the offices, walls, and people's desks look clean and neat. The change in their space has been profound. The energy and mood of the employees is different too, and more people fit into the same space without feeling crowded at all. That's been a particular bonus for them because they were actually considering a move to a bigger office space before the cleanup. Best of all, they were recently named the "best company to work for in British Columbia" by *BC Business* magazine and were also rated among the top seventy-five employers in Canada.

Get rid of private offices.

Open spaces create open work environments, and this leads to the development and transmission of office culture across people, departments, and finally, the entire organization. Years ago at the Junktion, we had all our employees on two wide-open floors. There were no walls. Then we moved into a downtown office tower and had to use the fourteenth floor of the building for the better part of a year while our real office space was constructed. For the first time ever, people had private offices, and it was interesting to see what happened. For the first week or so, people loved having their own space. They felt more focused, appeared to get more done, and had the quiet they needed to think. Then, after a week, the chatter started. People said, "I miss everyone," and, "Where is Steve? I haven't seen him in ages," or, "Is so-and-so sick today?" It went on and on. After about three weeks, it was unanimous: private offices killed the buzz and employees wanted their open work space back.

The benefits of open space are enormous in terms of better communication, better teamwork, better morale, and faster learning. Walls between staff are just that—barriers to teamwork; often, people are less productive because they can easily fart around during the day in privacy. Closed offices cause a ton of needless office politics. Avoid offices at all costs, even for execs.

And stop constructing silos. After you've gotten rid of private offices, make sure your employees aren't divided from one another by department either. Mix in sales with engineering, marketing with support. Not only will this build a positive culture, it will also enhance each employee's understanding of what other people in your company do. We had an employee who worked in the franchise sales area sit over in our compliance and operations departments for a few weeks. He began to hear and notice things related to how much waste we had in the company. He—and, subsequently, leadership—would never have noticed it as quickly if he'd been sitting in some private office.

How can you possibly be connected to your customers or your employees if senior executives are all on the top floor? Or if you're sitting in an office all day with the door closed? Don't remove yourself from the same space your employees occupy. By sitting with them in the same way as others, there won't be an us-them mentality, and you'll absorb the same work culture your employees do. Get rid of private offices.

Go (a little) crazy.

Nothing kills creativity in a new and exciting business more than boring photos on the walls or using super-traditional board and conference rooms. Go a little crazy and use the physical plant as a blank canvas to elevate the mood of the space. For example, at 1-800-GOT-JUNK? one of our boardrooms was called the Blue Sky Room. We had a huge wall painted with a mural of blue sky and clouds. It was beautiful. We also had a window that overlooked the North Shore Mountains. The light and airy mood these great visual elements created translated into happy employees. Don't be confined to some old-school vision of the workplace. You're not an old-school company. And you'll automatically have an advantage over employers who think statements such as "We have air-conditioning" will close the deal. Don't be afraid to go a little crazy.

Try to get outside the box a little and have fun with your office. One of the top advertising agencies in North America is called Rethink, and their boardroom table is actually a ping-pong table! They have green artificial turf as carpeting. These may seem like random additions, but by changing up the physical environment, they made a visual commitment to doing things differently. Employees are constantly reminded that their culture is different—all they have to do is take a look at their boardroom table to be reminded of that.

Brand everything. Give your meeting rooms names. Our offices at Ubarter.com had boardrooms named after the planets. The boardroom furthest from the CEO's office was called Pluto (at the time it was still recognized as the planet farthest from the Sun). Guests would always chuckle when they were told the meeting would be held in a room called "Neptune." If possible, engage all your employees in the naming process. Don't just slap a name on a boardroom without any employee input. Culture should flow from the inside out, not the other way around.

Make it easy to socialize. Some of you may balk at the suggestion to make it easier to socialize at your place of work, but it's a clever idea that will quickly help you develop a vibrant culture. Provide your people with a barbecue grill that is always kept clean and ready to use with propane so people can cook casually for lunch or dinner. This kind of interaction builds culture in an authentic and relatable way. With even less effort, have your kitchen stocked with free fruit, cereal, various coffees, teas, and more. You can even have the food delivered weekly by the grocery store. Whatever you do, make people feel at home. If you do, they'll work longer and harder for you.

In addition, try to set up a "Dream Room," a "Wii Room," and a "Nap Room" to take care of your employees who are working hard to build your dream. All of these little extras have to be genuine, desired, and used by everyone in the company to be effective.

Use your walls.

Put up huge positive sayings in vinyl letters or on canvasses you design. Pick words or sayings that mean something to your people, not obscure quotes that don't have any relevance to your team. This might not be possible right away, but as you cultivate real work culture, it'll be a lot easier to speak the language of your employees.

As I described in chapter 1, there's great value in putting up a "Can You Imagine?" wall. This should contain great ideas from your employees, customers, and suppliers. Fill the wall with ideas employees have for what your business looks like three years from now and check them off on the wall when they've been accomplished. Each little idea helps to share some of the employees' visions for the future of the company. Also include your company's core values on the wall so no one forgets them.

I have helped companies all over the world build their own Can You Imagine? walls. Many are twenty feet long and ten feet high. The visions of their employees, customers, and suppliers are approved by the CEO and then posted on the wall in large vinyl letters. Once they are achieved, they are checked off right there on the wall. These walls are highly effective when they are located near the lobby of the company for everyone to see. Some companies even have photos of the employees beside each one's vision instead of just listing the person's name. Their walls look awesome and really connect the vision to the people.

BE DIFFERENT: CREATING THE SOCIAL ENVIRONMENT

A company's physical environment, of course, is not enough to build a strong workplace culture. You have to create an outstanding social environment as well: one that will inspire everyone in your company to do their best—for themselves and for the team.

Creating a social environment means, uppermost, being different. I mentor a client in Toronto called I Love Rewards. Two years in a row, they've been ranked as one of the top companies to work for in Canada. They actually create rewards programs to help employers create great cultures for their own companies. Obviously, a company that's all about culture really "gets it."

One of the things I love most about I Love Rewards is that they have an employee area called the Red Point Lounge. Every Friday at 3:00 PM you can go have a drink there. Their company drink is called the Red Point, and it is served in these little crystal glasses with Red Point etched into them. All employees are given a stack of laminated cards that have the recipe for a Red Point drink on them. When they are out in the local pubs, they hand out drink cards to people and end up telling them about I Love Rewards. (A Red Point, by the way, is one and a half shots of Crown Royal, one and half shots of Sour Puss raspberry liqueur, and three shots of Red Bull. You have a couple of those and you're cranking out some extra work at the end of the day!)

The culture in your company may not be one that includes drinking together on a Friday afternoon, which is totally fine. I use this example simply to illustrate that a company's culture has to match what the CEO and the team are striving to build.

In addition, the folks at I Love Rewards don't take themselves so seriously that they can't have a little fun. They have white leather sofas in their office. They call their casual dress code "First-Date Dress Code"—in other words, if you wouldn't wear it on a first date, don't wear it to work. They get culture. No one quits at I Love Rewards.

Building Blocks of Creating the Social Environment

Along with striving to be different as a means of bringing your staff together, there are two pillars that support your social environment: hiring and communication. Without great people, you can't have a great culture, and effective hiring is the way to get great people. Communication is the glue of any social environment, both inside and outside of business. Open, honest communication is essential to building great teams and developing the kind of culture that will allow you to double the size of your business. Nothing in your company's culture can substitute for great communication.

Hiring and communication are so important and so complex that I have devoted entire chapters to these topics later in the book. For now, just remember that these are the basic building blocks of a powerful social environment.

Here are some specific ways you can develop the social environment in your company.

Build teams.

Don't underestimate the power of just hanging out with your employees. But you've got to do just that—*hang*. Don't turn the time into a business talk! Also, spend time with people who aren't your favorites. If you only hang out with the staff you're naturally drawn toward, then you'll continue to build walls within your teams that they see, but you don't. And that isn't good for you or your company.

When you're just spending time chatting casually with employees, you'll see they like that you're hanging out with them in an unstructured way. They'll start to open up to you as a person, and this will go a long way toward building the culture you want and achieving your Painted Picture. As you did while outlining action plans, think of the time you spend with employees as a dinner party: if you had a group of friends over for dinner, you'd chat with each of them and ensure they were having fun. Do the same at the office.

In my final years as COO at 1-800-GOT-JUNK? we had close to 240 employees at the headquarters. I no longer knew everyone's name. I was certainly beginning to spend more time with those who I knew and liked better. So, to try to bust through this a little bit, whenever I was heading out for lunch or coffee or leaving for the day, I would take a different exit path. Our office had three floors and covered about sixty thousand square feet. So I'd wander out between different rows of workstations, past different work areas, and just chat with people or say hi as I was leaving. I could always feel the energy among the people rise.

Force people to go home.

One of my favorite lines to use at the office was, "Great day—take the rest of it off." Sometimes I would tease people and say it at 6:00 PM. At other times, however, I'd say it to people at 10:30 AM and blow them away. Tell people to go home and relax once in a while. We all know that as entrepreneurs we duck out of the office for our little stress breaks. Let your team take some now and again too.

Give everyone five weeks' paid vacation.

When it comes to paid vacation, the United States doesn't get it, and frankly, Canada isn't much better. Giving only two weeks of paid vacation to employees says you're a mediocre employer, at best. Two weeks of paid vacation is particularly hard to swallow if you characterize your company as being "like a family." Really? Would you want your siblings or parents to have such little time each year to relax and restore themselves? You know that would really suck. So, *don't do it.*

European and Australian employers give five to six weeks' vacation, including sick days. The argument of many American businesspeople in the 1980s used to be, "Yeah, but look at the productivity of Americans, who have just two weeks of paid vacation!" They appeared to be judging countries that gave employees more time off as being lazy. But we can't in good faith argue that point anymore. Productivity has actually declined because we give our employees less and expect more, and that has to change.

To put it simply: the best companies, the companies attracting and retaining the most qualified employees, give more vacation than their mediocre counterparts. If you really want to be a great employer, here is one easy way to do it that doesn't cost you any more money than you spend on people today: give all of your full-time employees five (yes, five) weeks' vacation. Include sick days in those five weeks off. In addition to those five paid weeks' vacation, they obviously still get the other statutory government holidays like Christmas, New Year's Day, and so on.

Why does this work? Vacation time that includes sick days means employees won't come into work as often when they are sick. They know they have enough time off to cover those days, so they won't come in and infect everyone else. The number of sick days per year for your company will drop. You are also going to find that the only people who don't love this are the people who smoke or are unhealthy and perpetually sick, since they'll end up using much of their five weeks for sickness. Well, you don't want them on your bus anyway.

No one is going to quit. Why would they? Where else can they get such a great vacation package? With lower attrition rates and increased retention of employees, your employee training costs drop.

Everyone knows that the most productive day at the office is the day before vacation. So, the more vacation you give people, the more pre-vacation productivity gains you will see.

Also, you must give all employees the same vacation time. Otherwise, you're saying, "We like them more than we like you." Not a good move.

Educate employees on using their paid time off.

Teach your employees how to use their vacation time wisely. Don't allow them to carry days over to other years. The whole reason for giving five weeks' vacation is that you want people to take it so they perform at a higher level during the year. Let them know this is why you set paid time off this way.

Sometimes it's beneficial to give your people a little insight into how to structure their time off. I like to teach employees to split their five weeks' up like this:

- Two weeks—Use during summer holidays
- Five days—Spread during the period between Christmas and New Year's Eve. If they work the dates carefully, they can often set themselves up for close to two full weeks' off at year's end.
- One week—Use during late winter for a warm vacation or ski trip
- Five days—Spread over five long weekends by turning popular three-day holiday weekends into four-day breaks

Setting up vacations like this will really get your team relaxed, and they'll truly enjoy working for you.

Companies of all sizes, but especially smaller ones, should work to help employees cover their roles while they are on vacation. The common objection is "We can't offer so much time off because we don't have enough people to cover the roles; we're a small employer." Well, you have to cover for them when they are sick and during the two weeks of vacation they're allowed by law, so whatever you do in those situations you can easily do for a few more.

Work with the news media.

Work to secure awards and news coverage about all the great aspects of your company's culture. Get the media talking about you, and potential employees will flock to your organization. Look at every great company and you'll see how they've been able to get newspapers and magazines to write about such topics as alignment and empowerment of staff, creative work hours, results-only work environments, the funky furniture, the lack of private offices—the list is endless. This will also add to the positive emotional environment of your culture. Who wouldn't want to be part of a culture that's celebrated in the media?

In the early days of running College Pro Painters, I learned to get media coverage to attract customers and employees due to the culture of the painting company. While building 1-800-GOT-JUNK? we worked hard to get written up by the media and bloggers. We told them about the tours we'd take people on if they wanted to learn about our culture, and they frequently came. In fact, the more we told the media about our tours, the more people started coming to witness the awesome company culture they'd read or heard about. We fueled the buzz.

Companies like I Love Rewards, CityMax.com, Nurse Next Door, and RedBalloon all leverage their culture to generate free press about their company. It's been awesome to watch each of them rise through huge coverage about their culture. They've all been rated among the best companies to work for in Canada multiple times (except RedBalloon, which is based in Australia). Media coverage has added an aura to their culture and has actually helped build their culture by attracting applicants who are the perfect cultural fit.

EMPLOYEES' PERSONAL DREAMS

This next factor is so important in creating a dynamic and attractive social environment in your company I've given it a main heading all its own. Here's why.

A few years ago, I read a book called *The Dream Manager* by Matthew Kelly, and it blew me away. The general premise that I took away from this four-hour business-changing read is that if you care more about your employees' personal goals than the company work they are doing, they'll go through brick walls to help build your company. Sounds odd, but focusing on employees' dreams will change them forever, and they'll associate that positive feeling with your company.

How to Use Dreams

One easy, fun, and impactful system you can put in place is called the "101 Dream Goals." Give each employee thirty minutes to write down as many things as possible in these categories:

- The goods they'd like to buy

- The activities they'd like to do
- The subjects they want to learn
- The instruments or hobbies they want to learn
- The feats they want to try for the first time
- The personal goals they want to achieve
- The sights they want to see
- The places they want to go

Then start spending time every day or every week helping them make their dreams happen. Many of the things you do won't involve any time or money either. Employees will begin to feel a huge connection with you as you help them achieve their personal goals with nothing expected in return. When employees see the company really caring about them as people with dreams, some pretty awesome cultural stuff starts to happen. It's like the Law of Attraction. If people focus on what they want, they are less focused on petty things that frustrate them.

Let me give you an example. Three of my employees had student debt, and they felt like they were being crushed by it. They had no family support and no role models showing them how to get out of debt. The whole subject never would have come up had they not written "get out of debt" on their 101 Dream Goals lists. I asked the three of them if they were okay with me getting them all together to help them out. All expressed interest in meeting up. We set up a dinner club—I was buying—and for a few months we met to review budgets that included debt repayment, investing, and spending plans I put each of them on. Within six months, all were either out of debt or substantially on their way to getting out of debt. Two had started companies. All three were investing, and two were actually using my stockbroker as their adviser too. All were thrilled.

Another one of my employees, Geoff Coyle, wrote on his dreams list that he wanted to watch the Canadian National Hockey League team the Vancouver Canucks have a pregame practice and then to sit behind the players' bench to watch the actual game. For Geoff it seemed like an unattainable goal. However, I made one call to Mike Johnson, the assistant coach from the Vancouver Canucks, and he not only made it all happen, but a few of the players took Geoff out for drinks after the game. And yeah, Geoff would go through brick walls for me now, if you were wondering.

Many entrepreneurs say their employees are like family, but words are meaningless without actions behind them. When you really care for your employees like the family you say you are, that means caring for them personally and not just talking to them about what has to get done to build your company. A CEO with hundreds or thousands of employees can spur this movement by holding large group meetings or setting up a company website similar to 43things.com, where staff can share their goals. CEOs can start with one division at a time and let the idea of helping others' dreams become a reality spread throughout the company like a great virus. In fact, the more time a CEO spends caring about employees, the more time those employees will spend helping build the company for the CEO.

CREATING A CULTURE OF ENTREPRENEURSHIP

If you are building an entrepreneurial company, you need to build an entrepreneurial culture to go with it.

One way to create a culture of entrepreneurship is to treat all the employees as co-owners. Let them learn all the parts of a company and how it really runs. Share some of the profits of the company with them. Give them the same level of responsibility and accountability as the owner. Every one will begin to be excited about growth. Every one will start to treat the company as though they own it.

Share your financial statements with your employees, just as you share them with your co-owners. Don't worry that your employees will think you are making too much profit. When I share my financials with my friends (and employees), they understand the reality of the business. Instead of resenting me for all the money I make, they actually take responsibility for helping me grow the business.

When we ran a profit-sharing program at 1-800-GOT-JUNK?, one of the people who worked with us, Suzanne Paul (who made $42,000 a year), came to me one day with an idea to save the company money. "Do you know how much money we're spending on bottled water?"

I said, "No, I've got no idea."

"We're spending $500 a month on bottled water. That's $6,000 a year."

"Wow, that's a lot of money."

"Yeah, but I've found a better company who can come in and install these coolers with hot and cold filtered water and it will cost us only $100 a month instead of $500 a month. Can I do it?"

"Yeah, do it!" I replied.

"Great! I just wanted the rubber stamp; they're installing it tomorrow!"

Suzanne had already made the decision because of the profitability to "her" company's bottom line.

Years ago, I had another employee who walked around the office and stopped at each person's desk. She said, "I want you to open your desk drawers, take out all of the extra paper and pens and staples and Post-it notepads that you don't think you'll need for the next year, and place them all in this box." Some people had three boxes of staples, with five thousand in each box, in their desk. Who could ever go through three boxes of staples in a year? We had an entire year's worth of office supplies because this employee went around the office collecting stuff. She knew it would impact our profitability, and her actions were tied to us building a culture of entrepreneurship.

MAKE IT A CULT-URE

Let's stop and tally the results thus far. You're close to having a world-class work space—you've created the right physical environment, the right social environment, and a culture of entrepreneurship. These are great, but they're still not quite enough. To elevate your company to the level of the "zone of cult" you need to devote time to three more factors: energy, power, and authenticity.

Stir the Kool-Aid.

Years ago, my friend and brilliant speaker Jack Daly pushed me to ask myself every day, "What one thing did I do today to raise the energy level of my team?" When I think about it, it makes sense. The speed of the leader is the speed of the group. One of your jobs as a leader, no matter where you are in the company, is to raise the energy level of your team.

On the flip side, also ask yourself what you may have done to destroy the energy of the team. I distinctly remember the times I've taken an entire team and destroyed their energy and passion for days by saying the wrong thing or by publicly coming down on them. At times, I'd even feel myself doing it yet didn't stop. I had to learn how to listen to my conscience and let it guide me. Slowing down before saying something helped, but it was hard for me.

As you walk into the office each day, think about the things you can do to raise the energy in your workplace and team. Be yourself, but find ways to boost your employees every day. Find a way.

Create powerful meetings.

This is one of the keys to building a good culture. It is so important that, later in the book, I have dedicated a whole chapter to holding meetings. Just remember that your meetings are a reflection of your culture. You can't have a powerful and energetic culture without energetic and focused meetings. By focusing on meetings, you can elevate the strength of your culture as a whole.

Be authentic.

Culture is different for every company. You and your company might want to build a culture of innovation or fun or entrepreneurship or growth or respect—the list goes on and on. Being *authentic* is the one constant that works in each and every one of those cultures.

You need to build a culture and use the techniques outlined in this chapter that you feel comfortable with and that play to your strengths. Some leaders may be more of the rah-rah type, and they can lead the charge to create a culture with spirit and energy. Other leaders may not have this personality, but they can identify people in their companies who do and thus can enlist them to help motivate the team. Some leaders may be good in large groups, and others are better at relating to their employees one-on-one, over lunch or coffee. Given their own attributes, CEOs need to identify how they will best build and maintain a culture that is authentic and sustainable. Be careful not to be a leader who tries to "be the boss" or "dresses for success" instead of just being him- or herself.

—

Ultimately, each company will have its own way of building a unique culture. The important thing is not that they follow each step that I've discussed in this chapter; rather, they should build the people-centric culture I've described by using some or all of these tools in the context of their own strengths and weaknesses, their own likes and dislikes.

To wrap this up, I heard a *great* quote the other day, but for the life of me I can't recall who said it! "Culture trumps process any day." And it's true. I don't care how great your plan, financials, systems, or even people are. If you build a strong culture you'll overcome everything else. You will be able to double the size of your company in three years. Without a positive physical, social, and entrepreneurial culture, the rest doesn't much matter—or won't for long.

Now that you've got a full understanding of how important planning for fast growth is, it's time to take the second actionable step toward doubling the size of your company in three years: focus on building.

PART 2

FOCUSED ACTIONS FOR FAST GROWTH

CHAPTER 4

FOCUSED HIRING

"I am convinced that nothing we do is more important than hiring and developing people. At the end of the day you bet on people, not on strategies."
—Larry Bossidy, coauthor of *Execution*

Great people make great companies. Great people want to work with other great people. Positive people want to work with other positive people. And when you have great people who are positive about your company, you're on the fast track to doubling the size of your company in three years.

Assembling an awesome team takes work, though. As Jim Collins said in his book *Good to Great*, you've got to get the right people on your bus and the wrong people off your bus. This is especially true when it comes to cultivating the right culture in your workplace. At times you may not have to get the wrong people off the bus entirely; maybe they just need to be moved into a different seat. Once you put the right person in the right seat, you'll see the energy level increase.

In your Painted Picture, you probably have envisioned the perfect team, that is, employees you can trust to do an outstanding job and deliver the kind of results that will allow you to double your business. After all, your business is nothing but people. Without the right people, your business will not succeed. Focused hiring, therefore, is essential to making your Painted Picture a reality.

Whenever I discuss getting the right people, I think back on my time as president of Barter Business Exchange. While there, I hired a "Director of First Impressions." In typical business settings, this would be a receptionist or office manager. But since this wasn't a typical business setting,

I wanted someone whose positive energy would knock the socks off of any customers, suppliers, or employees as soon as they walked in the front door. Tina Etchart did just that. She nailed the first impression every time with her smile, awesome tone, and great energy. What first impression are you making at the front door of your offices? As the saying goes, you never get a second chance to make a first impression.

We used to have an internal mantra at College Pro Painters, UBarter.com, and 1-800-GOT-JUNK?: "raising the bar." The phrase was applied to both our external hiring processes and our existing team, and it inspired us to find new employees that raised the average skill set of the entire group. A business's hiring process is just like the process of rebuilding a sports team. You need to go in and, one by one, get rid of the wrong players and bring in those who raise the average of the team. A sports team would never consider bringing in a bunch of D-level players. Can you imagine players saying something like, "Let's get a couple of rookies on the team who aren't that good yet so we can play more!" On the contrary, every single player would obsess about bringing in *better* players because they all want a shot at winning the championship. Your company should be structured in the same way.

When a company is humming along, employees aren't pissed about their position or petty workplace issues. They are all excited to be chipping in and doing whatever it takes. You see it on championship sports teams all the time—guys sticking up for each other. Hire people with those traits.

Think about each piece of your organization as a little piece of a big puzzle. Each of your employees is also a piece of that same puzzle. You're going to see some who don't fit, and some who do. Over time you'll start pulling all the right puzzle pieces together. Even hires that were originally right can become the wrong employees as a company grows and changes. You don't want a static company; you want an evolving, organic one.

Jack Welch, former chairman and CEO of GE, was one of the greatest business leaders of all time. Every six months he'd review all of the people in the company and let them go if they didn't share the values that the organization stood for—*even* if someone was getting top results. If any individual was not in alignment with the rest of the organization and its values, he let that person go.

In this chapter, I'm going to give you tools that will help you get the right people into your organization and the wrong people out of it, so you can begin to *really* drive the business faster and further. But first, let's make a visit to my grandfather's duck blind.

A LESSON FROM DUCK HUNTING

I now realize that my grandfather, Cam Shortts, who recently died at the age of ninety-six, taught me how to hire great people when I was just a teenager. He owned a hunting and fishing resort in northern Ontario. Even though he was a business owner, the most important lessons I learned from him about recruiting happened while we were duck hunting, not talking business.

Let me repeat myself: I learned everything I know about recruiting amazing people from hunting ducks as a teenager with my grandfather—not from any book or classroom. Grandpa always knew exactly what kinds of ducks he wanted before we set out to hunt: blue-winged teals, mallards, wood ducks, and canvasbacks. He also knew what kind he didn't want: fish ducks. These fish-eating ducks don't taste nearly as good as other ducks. Before we set out on any hunting expedition, he made it clear what his goals were, and that our reward was only as worthwhile as the ducks we'd selected.

Recruiting the right people is just like duck hunting: you must have a crystal clear picture in your mind of exactly what you're looking for. You need to be sure that all new hires will truly impress every person they interact with, whether it's customers, strategic partners, vendors, the media, or the public at large. In other words, everyone you hire, from the front lines—sales and customer service—to the back office—accounting and IT specialists—must have the personality and skills to always exceed people's expectations.

When I joined 1-800-GOT-JUNK?, there were fourteen employees at our head office. When I left, we had more than 3,100 in total. How did we find the stars on our dynamic team? It all boiled down to what I learned duck hunting: before you get what you want, *you have to know what you want.*

FORECASTING HIRING NEEDS

Before we left to go hunting, Grandpa always reminded me that we were only allowed to shoot *six* ducks. So, six was the goal, but not just *any* six. They had to be the six very best ducks. He didn't want to use up part of our allotment on birds that wouldn't taste delicious.

How many employees do you need? When do you want them? Do you need to hire them all at once or spread them out over time? Perhaps at some point you'll want a few extra people. What happens if someone quits? What about temporary staff? What if your employees leave for another company? These kinds of thoughts and questions will arise with anyone who hires people. Regardless of what you're thinking, remember one thing above all else: if you scramble to hire, it's game over. You *lose*.

Have staffing plans and hiring needs mapped out at least one year in advance. In fact, when I was building 1-800-GOT-JUNK?, I had our staffing plans mapped by month, three years out. I knew every role we needed to hire for down to the month. We had to because we had six consecutive years of roughly 100 percent revenue growth.

Sometimes, however, in work life as in our personal life, John Lennon's adage "life is what happens to you when you're busy making other plans" applies. You're handed obstacles, and the time you're given to forecast and plan ahead is foreshortened. Here's a recent example to illustrate that very point.

This past summer I was mentoring Jason Lew, who runs Pine Village Preschool, a growing chain of bilingual preschools headquartered in Boston. He needed to hire twelve new teachers by the end of August. In our discussion I asked him a few questions: How many résumés do you think you need to net twelve hires? Where do you plan to get all the résumés you need? His answer to both questions was the same: he wasn't sure. Obviously, Jason needed some assistance.

During our discussions, Jason quickly realized that at each step of the process, a certain percentage of the applicants would drop out and not move to the next step. It turned out he would need 522 applications to end up with twelve qualified candidates to hire.

Then it got even more fun. I pointed out that in order to have the new hires ready to start on September 1, each new employee would have to go through two weeks of training, give his or her current employer notice, and perhaps take some summer vacation. We quickly realized that Jason needed to create a plan and then reverse engineer it to make it a reality. It was time to list, in order, every step in the recruiting process and assign a person to do each step. It was going to require military precision to generate that many résumés in time for the fall.

Here are the steps we listed in the recruiting process, which can apply to any business or organization no matter what its size.

- Applications
- Auto-reply
- Invitation to group interview
- Pass group interview
- Pass one-on-one interview
- Pass classroom test
- Pass reference checks
- CEO "sniff test"
- Offer accepted and signed
- Training

Another one of my clients wasn't caught off guard in their hiring forecast but nevertheless needed to create a list of recruiting steps just as Pine Village Preschool had. Rising Medical Solutions was in the process of hiring a vice president of sales. When I asked the hiring team to list all the things that had to happen before doing so, and put them in order, here is the list they ended up with.

- Scorecard for the role completed
- Job description written
- List of potential candidates put in writing
- Roles, goals, and expectations put in writing
- Networking for candidates started
- Compensation plan put in writing

- Job posting listed on key sites
- Recruiting firms engaged
- Interview questions written
- One-on-one interviews done
- Panel interview done
- Reference checks completed
- Background check completed
- Drug screening

I then asked them to carefully consider each step of the recruiting process. Each step had one employee who was assigned as the single point person accountable for completing it. More importantly, each step of the process had a date assigned to it. All Rising Medical Solutions had to do now was ensure that the employees responsible for a specific task had the skills and motivation necessary to complete it.

RECRUITING SUPERSTARS

When it came to hunting, I wasn't an awesome shot like Grandpa. I learned that if I wanted to shoot six ducks, I needed a lot more than six shells. I usually needed about twenty shells to get my six. Fortunately for me, when it came to business, I had much better aim.

A few years ago I was doing a talk for a group of CEOs at an Entrepreneurs' Organization event. One of them told me he couldn't hire any great employees because there weren't any available in his city. I said: "It's not a tight labor force. It's just that there are a whole bunch of shitty companies to work for. There are a ton of great employees; they just don't want to work for you. When you've become a great employer and you get your vision out there so everybody knows what you're building, that's when it's an easy market to find great employees."

When 1-800-GOT-JUNK? had been rated as the number-two company to work for in all of Canada (there were 1.46 million companies in the country at the time), we were averaging roughly 250 résumés for every position.

Keep looking.

Grandpa and I would wait patiently for the right ducks to fly by. To recruit remarkable people, I'm happy to wait.

No matter how tight the job market may seem, great employees still exist; they're just working somewhere else. Go out and poach them! And I'm not necessarily talking about picking up the phone and cold-calling them. The best way to grab great employees from another company is to be introduced to them by a mutual friend or acquaintance. LinkedIn and Facebook are great tools for finding people who might be able to make these introductions.

The only way to find the people who will help your business grow is to take a truly proactive approach. During a recent coaching call with a client who's a CEO in London, I made the comment that the best potential employees aren't looking for jobs. In fact, they're *never* looking for jobs because they've already got one. That's why you have to go out and poach them. In the thirty years of my professional life, I've had only two job interviews. The rest of the time I was poached by Company A while working for Company B.

The reality is that a lot of amazing employees are out there, but most of them are working for a lot of really average companies. Your job is to find the amazing people who are already working somewhere else and get them to work for you instead. You don't want to be recruiting and hiring people who are unemployed. You want to be recruiting and hiring people who are already working somewhere else. That's the key.

Bear in mind that A-level talent attracts A-level talent, whereas B-level talent ends up attracting C-level talent. Getting good people on board has a snowball effect. Be careless about hiring and you will quickly have a team of misfits. So, knowing this, I have always been on the prowl for A-level players. I'm constantly recruiting them, or I'm building relationships with them so I can recruit them later when I know spots are opening up.

Take, for example, the day Fortress Investment Group acquired Intrawest, a developer and operator of destination resorts. I was immediately on the phone with all the top people at Intrawest telling them I wanted to hire everyone who was great because the company was going to implode. I eventually hired five of their key people over the next three months because I knew that these people had already been working for a high-performance organization. I just went out and got them. It was as easy as that.

Never compromise.

I remember one particular trip I made with one of my directors to Boston. We were hiring for a position, but after three intense days of back-to-back interviews, we ended up flying home empty-handed. We interviewed sixteen candidates in multiple rounds of interviews. We combed through close to 150 résumés. Still, we walked away because we just didn't find the right person. Grandpa and I had days like that in a duck blind, but we never shot at fish ducks. We'd rather leave without a single duck than leave with a bad one.

If I don't find precisely the person I want, I keep looking. There are more than 300 million people living in the United States, and the right people exist for every role. You just have to keep looking. Trust your gut: when it says no, don't let yourself keep trying to make it say yes. It's always better to keep looking than to settle for a B player.

INTERVIEWING FOR GREAT PEOPLE

Hunters can easily identify the best ducks, and they never shoot at the fish-eating ducks. Grandpa could pick the best ducks out in the sky, even when they were at a distance. He knew just by their silhouettes and the speed of their wings flapping. It was eerie. Grandpa would often point to the sky and say, "Look, some ducks!" I would eagerly scan the horizon and then ask, *"Where?"* Grandpa was patient, and eventually, as they drew nearer, he'd point out a mallard or two and a green-wing teal. Lo and behold, after we'd shot them or they'd flown past, I knew he'd been right. I, on the other hand, could barely tell that they were ducks. Granted, Grandpa owned a hunting resort, so he had plenty of practice. However, most importantly, he really knew without question what he was looking for and could pick it out from a mile away.

Our company can spot the ducks we want—even if they're flying way off in the distance—by following several steps that lead up to a group interview.

When an application is emailed to us for a job posting, an auto-reply sends the applicant an email that says: "Thanks for applying to work for us. Please read our Painted Picture, which is attached. It explains what our company will look and feel like three years from now. If this sounds like the kind of company you want to help build, please reply to this email with 'Interview me' in the subject line."

Our Painted Picture, therefore, begins attracting the right people and repelling the ones who wouldn't work well with us. Right from the start, prospective employees know whether they fit the company or not.

If I want to hire six people, I need to review more than six résumés and interview more than six candidates. Build the number of résumés and interviews required for each person you want to hire into your recruiting plan. To hire one truly remarkable person, I like to interview at least five to eight people. However, we often interview many more to find truly stellar individuals. On average, I've had 250 résumés and conducted sixteen interviews to hire just one person.

Instead of using the one-on-one interview format, all of our interviews are conducted simultaneously in the same room. This makes it easier to determine the best cultural fit and to see who has the leadership traits we value most in a group setting. The results have been outstanding.

Group Interviews

In the mid-nineties, I learned about a company called Mad Science out of Montreal that had created a unique group-interview process. It consists of bringing eight candidates into a boardroom for sixty to ninety minutes. The candidates are told they'll be participating in a group interview in advance and are then briefed on the group-interview process before starting. Then someone from the hiring company asks the candidates simple questions such as these: What books do you read? What do you do for fun? What's your favorite movie?

What was the most stressful time in your life? Who's the best candidate in the room, and why? And so on. Advise the candidates that this interview is a "lightning round" of sorts, and be sure to tell them that you may be cutting them off once you've heard what you need to hear from their responses. A candidate should never be made to feel foolish, however. It's a balancing act.

Every candidate answers each of the simple introductory questions, but you rotate the order in which the responses are given—that is, let each person go first and last. In this situation, speed is your friend; you want to cut the candidates off with a simple, "Okay, thanks," and then move on, but don't be disrespectful. This makes the process more like a fun test rather than a stiff interview. You'll get more authentic responses, too, because people tend to let their guard down after a while.

Usually you need to keep the entire group for the whole ninety-minute period, but a couple of times when we had four extremely poor candidates and we wanted the other four hot ones to know we were serious, we said: "Okay, that's been three questions, and now we'll ask one more in the first round. Then we're going to eliminate some candidates and ask those of you who we think should stay five more questions."

This group interview process cuts down on the overall time spent on the hiring process. Not only do you save time hiring from your office, it also makes it particularly advantageous for hiring in other cities and with large numbers of candidates who require second and third rounds of questioning.

Here are some of the questions I typically use during group interviews. Keep in mind that I'm only looking for cultural fit and leadership at this stage.

- What are your favorite books and magazines, and why?
- What is your favorite movie, and why?
- What car is most similar to you as a person, and why?
- What was the most stressful time of your life, and why?
- What was the most complex project you ever led, and why?
- What stresses you out?
- Why do you want to work here?

- Who is the best candidate in the room, and why?
- If we were to hire two people, and you were one of them, who would you want us to hire to work with you?
- When could you start, and how much do you need to earn during year one? Year three?

I love this last question because candidates will actually give you the real dollar amount they'd work for versus an inflated number they'd give if no one else were around.

If you follow this process properly, you won't overlook star candidates whose résumés you've already reviewed prior to inviting them to the group interview. Remember, the purpose of the group interview is to screen for cultural fit and leadership—that's what gets candidates into a second interview.

I like to compare this process to a similar practice Steve Jobs initiated at Apple. He'd show a prototype of the Mac computer to prospective employees, and if he couldn't see the sparkle in their eyes when they first saw it, he didn't bother interviewing them any further.

When Steve Jobs and Steve Wozniak started Apple, they knew exactly what they were looking for in their employees. They hired people who wanted to challenge the status quo. They hired people who wanted to empower the human race. They weren't just about making computers. Steve Jobs wanted to put a dent in the universe, and he hired people who could help Apple achieve that goal.

Hire people who are passionate about their work. Hire people who have deep passions outside of work. And when prospective employees say things like, "I just want in," and "You're the *only* company I want to work for," you know you're on the right track.

The old adage "hire for attitude, train for skills" doesn't work in the new fast-paced environments we work in these days. Many CEOs are starting to realize this, but only after learning it the hard way. A good attitude can't overcome a lack of skills, and when you're growing at 100 percent revenue growth a year for six consecutive years, you have to be able to bring in the kind of people you know will be able to get the job done right away. What should you do? Go out and attract résumés from the best people who already have proven skills. Then, ensure that they also have the great attitude through the group-interview process. (You'll be making sure they really do have the necessary skills through a one-on-one interview.) Often you and your company aren't equipped to train people anyway, so hiring proven talent will fast-forward you.

The final way to safeguard against overlooking a star candidate is to really push hard to find two hundred résumés for every single position for which you want to hire, then narrow that group down to sixteen or so. That's when you'll find the A-level players. If there is a destructive person in the group interview who clearly doesn't measure up, you can always ask him or her to leave. Just be polite and considerate, and don't use it as an opportunity to embarrass the individual; that reflects negatively on you and your organization.

In a group interview of eight, you'll usually find two to three candidates with whom you'll want to do more in-depth interviews.

One-on-One Interviews

The group interview serves as a way for you to screen for cultural fit and leadership. The two-hour second interview is where you grill the candidates and find out whether they have the skills required for the position in question. A third interview, with additional people from your organization, is where you test your conclusions about the candidates.

One of the most important lessons I've learned from interviewing is that everyone lies or, at the very least, exaggerates a little bit. When you're interviewing people, you must make sure that candidates actually have experience doing what they say they do. You want to find people that have *proven past performance*.

I'll give you an example. Years ago, I was looking for an expert in time management, someone who could serve as a role model for others in the group. One candidate I interviewed was very impressive, and he began talking to me about his theory of time management. The way he was talking to me, he could have written textbooks on time management and related topics. He was just perfect, or so I thought.

But then a funny thing happened. When I started grilling him and asking for examples of how he put his theory into practice, I had a gut feeling he himself didn't really use any of these time management techniques.

So I said, "Well, do you use a Day-Timer?" (This was back before PDAs, and Day-Timers were all the rage.)

"Oh yeah. I use a Time Text. I've been using it for years."

"Do you do everything you just described to me using that?" I asked.

"Yeah, totally," he responded.

I then asked him if he had his Time Text on him, and he told me he didn't bring it to the interview, but he never left home without it. So I asked him where his Time Text was at that very moment, and he said it was in his car. I then asked him if he wouldn't mind running out to his car to grab it. He willingly got up from the interview and went out to his car to get it. And I never saw him again!

The moral of this story is that there are a lot of people who talk a good game but don't know how to put theory into practice. You want employees who have practiced and perfected their craft. Your business deserves nothing less than people who are fantastic cultural fits, are strong leaders, have proven ability to perform their roles, and will do it at one hundred miles an hour.

Guidelines for Conducting Interviews

Employees at your company who are doing the one-on-one interviews need to know how to balance interviewing and rating a candidate using a "Top Grading" scoring system (I'll provide details about this system a little further on) with selling the candidate on joining your company (without appearing like they're giving them a "hard sell"). When the interview is conducted properly, it may get intense. So what? If the candidate is given the job it will be way more intense than the interview anyway. You need to know prospective employees handle the pressure. That said, the interviewing employee should never be disrespectful to the candidate.

You can facilitate the in-depth interviewing process by walking your employees who will be involved through the following steps.

Preparation

As with any business event, preparation is critical. In preparing for the interview, you should review each candidate's résumé and dig around on Facebook, LinkedIn, and Twitter (or any other social media sites) to learn more about the person there. Formulate a list of questions related to the preferences and abilities you've already decided you need in a candidate. (See the section on page 74 called "Behavioral Traits to Look for During Interviews" for more details about rating these attributes.) Your preparation should yield a list of areas to delve into deeper. I love writing my questions right on the résumé and then, once I've got a ton of questions written down, putting a number beside each in the order I'll ask them; this ensures that I have time to cover them all.

Remember, the purpose of the interview is to determine the probability of the candidate's success in the position for which they're interviewing. The better prepared the interviewer, the greater the likelihood of making that determination.

One-on-one interviews should always be two hours and can often go as long as four hours if you've really prepared and really grill the candidates, asking multiple questions in each area.

Setup

Use your intuition to know whether a relaxed or more formal atmosphere is appropriate according to the role, level of position, and company culture you're building. For many roles, doing interviews at a coffee shop is fine; for others, a boardroom setting is a must. When hiring employees who will work remotely in another area of the country, you won't be interviewing them at your offices, so think about finding a location for the interview that suits the role and the company's culture even though you're not in your home city.

The Process

Before you go into the interview, be sure you have all of your notes on the candidate, his or her résumé, and any other useful documents. Strive to build rapport with the candidate. Ask your questions directly and clearly. When candidates answer a question but you don't fully understand their response, follow up by asking them to elaborate. Ask about the mentors they turned to for advice, how they made decisions, and what influenced their decisions. Balance being assertive in obtaining the answers you need with being respectful of the applicant.

Always look for transition points in the candidate's job history, because that's where the most illustrative stories lie, and if a candidate shares them, you'll begin to see more of him or her as a person. (If a candidate hesitates to share these details, that reveals a great deal too.) Evidence of moving—either frequently or rarely—between jobs, schools, careers, or marital statuses helps you get a better idea of the candidate's character. Probe into the transitions—respectfully—and find out why they happened. Don't assume all transitions are bad; ask the candidates why they made the choices they did in order to get a comprehensive picture of them as an individual.

Here's a list of "probing" questions about areas of concern or red flags that will help you elicit the information you'll need. (For still more interview questions, refer to appendix 1 at the back of the book.)

- What made you choose that area of study in university?
- Who influenced you in leaving your last career?
- How were you feeling at your last company when (insert some situation that the candidate may have mentioned or that you gleaned from the person's résumé or news coverage about the company or industry) happened?
- Why do you let everyone else tell you what to do? (You might ask this if you notice the applicant lacks promotions or leadership roles.)

Interviewers should spend 80 percent of the time listening. When you hear yourself telling a story or talking about the company, stop and get the candidate talking again. The purpose of the interview is to find out about a prospective employee, not to tell the interviewee about you.

Use pregnant pauses to get candidates to reveal more. Every so often count to ten in your head after candidates have already given their answer and watch how much more detail they volunteer to fill the silence. When the subject is of particular importance, pause again and listen until the candidate has nothing left to share.

Take proper notes throughout the interview and record a rating from 1 to 5 for each area of experience and skill set (again, see "Behavioral Traits to Look for During Interviews" on page 74). Each of your ratings must be supported by three reasons from the candidate's past work performance or life history. If you rate a person a 5 in Attainment, for example, your three solid, irrefutable reasons that uphold that rating would be something like these:

- They set and write down personal goals on a weekly basis; they have them on a piece of paper in their wallet for the last three weeks of the month. They are crossing them off, too, as each goal is met.
- They mention setting goals for running half marathons the following summer, and they already know all the split times they'll need in order to hit their goal time of an hour and thirty-five minutes.
- They have a retirement-age goal of sixty and explain in detail how they'll have saved enough money to retire at that age and pay their living costs until dying at 100. (In the interview in which the candidate shared this, her plan was so detailed that I was taking notes for myself.)

During the interview, remember to silently ask *yourself* some questions and interact with what each candidate is telling you.

- Do I know enough about this person to make a decision yet?
- What is bothering me about this person's work history/educational background/attitude that I haven't probed into yet?
- Does this person put me at ease, or am I on edge?
- Have I maintained control of the interview, or has the candidate shifted the roles?
- Would I like to have this person to my home for dinner with my best friends?
- Is the candidate a good listener? Would he or she be a cooperative team player?

Focus on the decisions the candidates have made in the past. Making decisions means making choices, and choices show you people's values and preferences (although not everything is as it seems, which is why you probe). Your interview should be tough, pointed, and probing.

Selling

During the interview process, you should use a technique that I call the "reverse sell." It involves being in a position of power throughout the interview and getting candidates to sell themselves on joining your company and sell you on their ability to handle the job.

As you use the reverse selling technique, emphasize how hard a position will be and see how the candidate reacts. You should also state the concerns you might have about some of the person's weaknesses and having the person address them on the spot. For example, you might say, "It appears your computer skills are very poor and will hurt you. Can you speak to that issue?"

Address any concerns or fears the candidate has, but don't handle them as they come up during the interview. Instead, hold their concerns or fears in the back of your mind until just the right moment later on. Then handle them thoroughly so the candidate isn't worried about them.

When the interview is over, if the candidate is more excited than ever, really believes he or she can do the job, feels raked over the coals a bit, and feels that he or she might not get the offer, then you've done your job.

Closing

Throughout the interview, have the candidate write down any random questions that come to his or her mind and say that you'll get to them later. Then, during the closing of the interview, make sure you give the candidate a chance to ask those questions. Likewise, make doubly sure that all of your questions have been asked. Leave no stone unturned. If you discussed the need for additional information, remind the person to send those supplementary documents via email or the post. You should also lay out for the candidate the next steps that will happen in-house and when they can expect to hear from you.

At the end of the interview, ensure that you have collected all the information you need for the debriefing you'll have with colleagues so you can support each of the ratings you have given the candidate. You have to be comfortable with your "go/no-go" decision. Be prepared to explain your decisions to other individuals in your organization who will have interviewed the same candidates.

Behavioral Traits to Look for During Interviews

What follows is a list of traits you should be looking for when you interview a candidate. I suggest you pick ten critical ones and focus on those. To help you make that determination, I've put an asterisk beside the traits I always focus on during any interview.

- Attainment/focus on goals (*)
- Decision making
- Interdependence
- Introspection (*)
- Leadership (*)
- Organizational skills (*)
- People/interpersonal skills (*)
- Ability to handle pressure (*)
- Sales ability
- Tenacity (*)
- Values (*)
- Assertiveness
- Coaching ability
- Ability to handle conflict (*)
- Customer service
- Emotional intelligence (*)
- Patience
- Analytical skills
- Communication skills (written and verbal)
- Diplomacy skills
- Listening skills
- Negotiation skills
- Precision/attention to detail (*)
- Problem-solving (*)

- Resourcefulness
- Willingness to take risks
- Ability to work as part of a team
- Technology skills (*)
- Work-life balance
- Ability to delegate
- Job knowledge
- Management of change
- Strategic thinking
- Creativity
- Imagination
- Inventiveness

Rating Guide

Statistically, out of every group of ten people you interview, only one of them should have a 5 (the highest value) in each of the areas you are using to profile them and only one of them should have a 1 (the lowest value). (Note that no half points are allowed in this rating system.) On average, two of the ten will be given a 2 rating and another two candidates a 4. The majority, four of the ten candidates, will be assigned a 3. If you find yourself rating all the candidates the same, force yourself to get more realistic with your ratings. By implementing this rating process rigorously, you won't let average candidates slip by because you rated them too high.

FIRING IS AS IMPORTANT AS HIRING

I once had a mentor who asked me, "Do you have any of the wrong people in your company?"

"Yeah, I've got one guy," I replied.

"How long have you known he's the wrong person?"

"I've known for about six months."

"Why haven't you let him go?"

"Because he's the guy who got some big PR for us; because he's been really good for the last couple of years; because I really like him and he really cares."

"Why do you want to let him go then?"

"Well, he's an emotional wreck . . ."

I rattled off all these reasons and incidents that revealed why the company needed to let him go, and when I was finished, my mentor looked at me and said, "I need you to tell me the date that you're going to fire him."

"Okay, I'll let him go by Friday." This was a Tuesday morning, at a Denny's on Broadway in Vancouver.

"So you'll let him go by Friday?"

"Yeah, Friday."

"That's not good enough."

"Okay, I'll let him go Wednesday."

Then he just stared at me and said, "Chicken!"

"Okay, I'll let him go *today*."

"Good. What time?"

This was 7:30 in the morning. I'd just moved the firing from someday to Friday to Wednesday to the very same day, and now he wanted to know what *time*? So I said, "I'll do it by noon."

My mentor nodded and wrapped up the conversation. "Good. Call me at 12:05 PM and I'll be there for you. But you make damn sure you're there for him. You make sure when you're getting this person off your bus that you respect him and his integrity. You treat him like a person; you mentor him to help him grow in the next phase of his career. You have an obligation to him, because six months ago is when you should have let him go, and for the last six months you've been stealing from him. He didn't want to quit because of you; he wanted to be there to be loyal to you, and because you were too chicken to let him go six months ago, when you should have, you've taken six months of his life. So you make sure that you're there for him."

That was some of the hardest-hitting and best teaching I've ever had in business. I had put off talking to my friend and justified the delay to myself using all the excuses. Having my mentor hammer it into me really ate away at me. Hard to hear, easy to execute. I met with the employee after that breakfast. We both cried when I had to let him go that day.

Five years later, I still get emails and Facebook messages every week or two from the guy saying: "Hope you're well. How are the kids? How are your travels?"

The moral of this story is that you simply must get the wrong people out of your organization in the right way in order to build a powerful culture. If you remove people from your organization in the wrong way, you'll destroy your culture. This was one of the hardest yet most inspiring moments of all my years in business.

—

Focused hiring, and even more focused firing, will allow you to assemble a team with the ability to support your company's growth. Once your team is in place, communication is the key to putting the team into action.

CHAPTER 5

FOCUSED COMMUNICATION

"The single biggest problem in communication is the illusion that it has taken place."
—George Bernard Shaw

Communication is difficult. To prove my point, try reading the next sentence six times, and put the emphasis on a different word each time.

"**I** Didn't Say You Were Beautiful."

"I **Didn't** Say You Were Beautiful."

"I Didn't **Say** You Were Beautiful."

"I Didn't Say **You** Were Beautiful."

"I Didn't Say You **Were** Beautiful."

"I Didn't Say You Were **Beautiful**."

If this set of six words can mean so many different things, it's no wonder that communication within a company can be so confusing and frustrating at times.

A good friend of mine once asked me, "Are you arguing to be right or are you trying to be understood?" Over the years, I've asked this question more and more to remind myself that the key to good communication is *listening* to what people have to say, not telling them what you need to get done. Communication isn't a one-way street: you can't bark orders and commands and expect all employees to follow them. In fact, that technique may even be wildly detrimental to what you're trying to accomplish with your business.

To communicate effectively, you have to focus on making others understand your message. You also have to make sure that everyone in your company can communicate with one another and the outside world.

This chapter is about the tools, techniques, and attitudes you need in order to communicate effectively. It's also about making good communication a priority for your business, not just a part of assigning tasks and managing people.

BIG-PICTURE COMMUNICATION ISSUES

"God gave you two ears and one mouth; use them in that ratio."

I used to think this common saying was only applicable to leaders, but as I began writing this chapter, it dawned on me that it can be applied to anyone operating within a company. The point is that we need to listen twice as much as we talk. Too many of us race to get our two cents in, trying desperately to be heard without first hearing what others are saying.

"Seek first to understand, then to be understood," wrote Steven Covey, bestselling author of *The Seven Habits of Highly Effective People*. Often the key to great communication is simply listening—and I mean *really* listening—to what the other person has to say and waiting to respond once you've digested what they've said.

If you want to have an open work culture and a respectful workplace, or if you're trying to get employees to come to you with problems or opportunities, the first thing you need to do is master listening. I simply can't emphasize how important this is. After you've listened, ask questions so that you understand exactly what the other person is saying. Then take twenty-four hours to respond—if possible—so that you have time to really absorb what was said. With all of your personal strength, resist the urge to shut anyone down, because once you do, that employee will never come back to you with his or her problems or suggestions on how to make your company better.

Why is this so important? Well, it goes back to my good friend's question to me about whether I was fighting to get my point across because I wanted the validation of being "right" or because I passionately wanted to explain myself. It's a hard question to answer, but here's a hint: if you're communicating with others only to tell them how you want things done, you're not communicating effectively.

Communication starts when information and feedback are allowed to flow freely, without fear of professional repercussions or judgment. People want to be heard—*listened* to—and require thoughtful responses, not curt corporate-speak. In the end, this combination of listening, openness, and trust will be the best way to achieve the kind of communication that will make your Painted Picture a reality.

Let's discuss the steps you need to take in order to build the kind of company you envision. The first step is the most physical of all these tips for communication. The rest are much more subtle, so pay attention.

Get out of your offices.

I already mentioned this as part of creating a physical environment for a positive corporate culture, but it applies here just as importantly. To vividly demonstrate to your employees that you are committed to excellent two-way communication, get rid of the private offices in your work space. Seriously. While this isn't the only way to show you are committed to the free flow of information, I believe it's a powerful way of setting the stage—so to speak—for your employees to pick up on the significant role free-flowing information and feedback play in success.

When I was a little kid in Winnipeg, Canada, I attended the city's first "open concept" school, which meant that there were no classrooms, no walls, and lots of great buzz. Sure there were lots of distractions, but there was lots of absorbing of what others were doing, too. From this experience, I learned how to focus when I had to and also how to ferret out what I could learn from those around me.

Building an open office doesn't mean that the employees work out in the open while the CEO and other senior staff retreat to private offices. Everyone has to be out in the open—and I mean *everyone*. Of course, you can still have groups of people separated from others by glass walls in some areas. For example, why not create the "Finance Fishbowl" and put all the finance people in one area and give them a glass wall if needed.

You can also go radical and have the only barriers around workstations be forty-two-inches high—that's only three and a half feet—so you really aren't blocking much at all. Everyone will be able to see everyone, which means no hiding. If you aren't working, it'll be obvious.

The benefits of an open work space are numerous. For starters, open offices teach you to filter out the noise and still concentrate on your work. They also allow everyone to hear what's going on, which means they'll understand others' roles better. Best of all? You'll feel the energy and togetherness grow within the company because you can see everyone more than when they are hiding out in walled offices. Don't worry; if you want to have private work areas, spots to take confidential phone calls, or little places for private discussions, you can still have lots of small meeting rooms. But whatever you do, get out of your offices!

Have an open-door policy.

As with offices, communication needs to be open. What does that mean, exactly? For starters, it means no hidden agendas, and it means you share more than the bare minimum of confidential information with everyone. The more open the communication is across individuals and departments, the more trust will be built within the company and its teams.

Communication has to flow top-down, bottom-up, and between peers and business areas. It's not always easy to make this happen, but one of the most effective ways I've been able to maintain this flow of communication is to have an open-door policy. Even though, technically, if you have no walls you won't have doors, the phrase encapsulates the approach all leaders should take to fielding people's opinions and concerns. It shows everyone that the people in charge are willing to grab some time to listen to the creative ideas as well as the problems, fears, and frustrations that are percolating throughout the organization. For example, when I worked at 1-800-GOT-JUNK?, Kurt Comer, who used to work on our call center sales floor, would grab me with some idea at least once or twice a month, even though there were three layers of management between Kurt and me. It helped that he was our top salesperson and that he was fun to be around, but his comments weren't always easy to hear. Being open to him sure helped, though. From time to time, Kurt would also help me share what I needed to communicate with hundreds of other agents as well.

"Town hall" style meetings also helped with the flow of communication out to large numbers of people and back to me. These communication extravaganzas were set up as an open forum, usually with a few beers being passed around to get people relaxed, and they allowed for the top-down, bottom-up flow of information I mentioned earlier. Most importantly, leaders have to "walk the walk" in this context. You have to be prepared to show people you're working to resolve issues they've brought to your attention or to shine a spotlight on any of the areas that need one. That's what it means to lead.

Fostering outstanding communication within your company need not be limited to large-scale efforts like tearing down walls and having town hall–style meetings, however. One of the most impactful things we did to foster good communication at 1-800-GOT-JUNK? and at companies I have mentored since was running the "daily huddle" (check out chapter 6 on focused meetings for more about this type of gathering). The power of sharing good news, releasing the key numbers, getting updates from different business areas, and even hearing reports of missing systems we needed or frustrations employees were having each day really allowed everyone to get on and *stay on* the same page. Everyone knew what everyone else was doing, and why it was important.

Be open to criticism.

When I was COO of 1-800-GOT-JUNK?, we worked hard to foster an open work culture and to build real trust between one another. Our bond was so strong that at our seven-minute huddle meeting at 10:55 AM each day, we finished by asking, "Are there any missing systems or key frustrations?" People would put their hands up and say things like, "Something's broken," "This isn't working," or "I don't like the way this is happening." However they phrased it, employees felt safe enough in that environment to speak openly about problems or areas of concern so that they could resolve the issue or, at the very least, make the situation better. And that's precisely what you want.

No matter how amazing your business is, you're never immune to failure; sometimes things just don't work. As an entrepreneur running a healthy business, your challenge isn't to dread those inevitable failures but to implement processes that help you deal with them so that they ultimately make your business stronger. I've learned from *The E-Myth* by Michael Gerber that people don't fail, *systems* do. Strive to reinforce that message so well that your people are willing to point out what is broken and are sure that they aren't going to get blamed or sacked by one of the executive team or their boss for saying so.

Learn to react fast.

React fast to the information you receive, but don't overreact. It's a delicate balance, but you've got to do it. I've often seen people sit on bad news without making the appropriate changes. I've found it's equally bad to sit on great news and not leverage it or praise people. Employees who look to you for guidance, inspiration, and leadership get frustrated when they give you real information and you're completely paralyzed and unable to do anything about it.

Practice nonpartisan conflict management by racing to the conflict.

"Race to the conflict" is one of the first management phrases I learned back in 1986 while I was with College Pro Painters. The key to this was to realize that when something bugged me, it was important to act on it right away—but never in writing. I learned that it is always better to confront the matter in person. Employees respected me for handling situations this way; it built trust and meant nothing was left to fester. Also, addressing the matter in person allowed the other party or parties to share their thoughts on the matter too. Sometimes their perspective gave me a lot of additional information I thought I had, but that I definitely didn't.

Before racing to the conflict, however, I advise you to take some time to let yourself defuse a bit. Go for a quick walk, do twenty push-ups, grab some water, breathe, or find some other way to relax yourself. Don't take too long, but ensure that you've calmed down before you meet with the party or parties involved.

Here's a great model I learned at that time that will help you deal with conflict when it arises in your workplace.

Often the hardest part of dealing with conflict is removing the emotions that entangle it and surfacing the issue underlying it. Conflict, by nature, involves emotions, and oftentimes those emotions take on more importance than the issue itself. A great way to deal with both the emotional and the objective side of conflict is to get all the issues out on the table to be discussed in an impartial way.

Define the problem.

Deal with the reason the person brought up the conflict and the underlying issues. Try not to get too personal, and be sure to stay on track. Remember, you are confronting the issue, not the person. Examine what you did that might have contributed to the problem. Take the lead and admit the things you did that were wrong. Explain what you could have done differently and encourage the other person to do the same. Acknowledge what each person wants out of the process of airing the conflict. Good conflict management means getting each person to admit his or her contribution, view of the facts, and feelings.

Actively verbalize your side.

I've found that using the following phrases really helps in communicating effectively when you're trying to resolve a conflict. You don't have to use the exact phrases, but they do help frame the discussion so that you ultimately arrive at the desired outcome.

"When you . . ." Describe exactly what the person did that you didn't like, or what the person did that doesn't follow your system, values, and so on. Don't criticize the person; criticize his or her actions. Be descriptive, not evaluative.

"I feel . . ." Tell the person how his or her actions make you feel.

For example, "I feel upset, frustrated, angry." Describe your feelings and dig deep. If you can truly express your emotions, you'll have no problem addressing the problem itself.

"I need . . ." Describe what you need the person to do in the future in these situations so the conflict doesn't return. By focusing on this, you've addressed your feelings and the person realizes you are getting to the meat of the issue and focusing on getting the problem solved.

"How do you feel?" Ask the other person to put his or her thoughts and feelings on the table. The other party likely has feelings, emotions, and a version of the facts that need to be heard and validated before the conflict can be resolved. If you don't allow others to articulate their feelings and impressions of what happened, the conflict won't get resolved.

Actively listen to the other side.

Active listening is crucial to understanding what the other person is saying. During this process, the other person must feel that you are empathizing with him or her and that you understand and care about his or her point of view. To really help you with this, use techniques such as paraphrasing, that is, repeating back what was said and asking if you understood correctly. You can also use "perception checking," that is, the process of watching the other party's reaction and asking whether he or she is following you and understanding what you're saying.

Outcome

At the end of the session ask yourself, have emotions been diffused and has an agreement been made on the issue? This is a real bobbing and weaving process that can be complex. You need to be assertive in wanting to reach a win-win solution. Repeat the rounds of active verbalizing and active listening until you've reached agreement on how to solve the conflict.

Learn to be a coach.

Coaching and developing people is core to a leader's role, and it requires communication. I can't recall where I heard this, but the phrase "the ability to get people promoted is the best sign of a great leader" couldn't be more accurate.

Coaching done well is an *art*, and therefore it requires training.

The best athletes in the world have coaches, and they still learn from them even at the top of their game. Employees in a growing organization need the same skill development. Learning how to adapt our coaching styles to different situations and give constructive guidance and feedback are important every day because they force us to process information and then turn that information into action. We spend time coaching employees in a business setting because we need our learners to increase their results so we can hit our goals. At the end of the day, coaching will assist us in hitting the results *we* are supposed to hit, too, because we're communicating our vision, our Painted Picture for our organization.

There is no question that preparation is one of the most important areas of coaching. If not done properly, the coach is merely flying by the seat of his or her pants—and the learner knows this. As a leader, you know full well how your time gets stretched with the number of subordinates you have reporting to you. Experts commonly recommend a maximum of eight direct reports, and from my experience, eight seems to be pretty accurate.

Become a communicator who excels in giving feedback.

Communicating feedback to employees is all about learning. Remember, however, that those who are learning control the learning environment, and they have to want to learn in order to be successful. If they don't want to learn, they won't. The learner must perceive a need for acquiring new knowledge; if the learners already think they know it all, they won't be ready to learn from you. Let them create their own need by failing a couple of times.

Feedback can be either written or verbal. I use both. Usually a mix of clear, concise written feedback that incorporates comments about where an employee can improve, along with affirmation of areas in which he or she should continue what's being done, works best. Scoring each area on a scale also works in clarifying the feedback. Feedback has to be accurate; it should show that you observed your employees closely and took good written and mental notes about their performance. It is much better to say *exactly* what was done well or what could be improved upon. By providing specific examples, your employees know exactly where to focus their efforts in order to improve.

As a general rule, people enjoy getting positive feedback and don't like hearing too much negative feedback. Providing positive feedback shows support for their efforts and fosters more open learning. Often, when you address people's strengths, the flip side is a weakness that they will notice on their own. Start your feedback with positive statements. As I like to say, "two strokes for one poke," meaning we give them two positives they should maintain for each negative they have to work on.

Keep in mind that the message delivered isn't always the message received. Ask your employees to repeat back to you the feedback you just gave them. Not only does this practice ensure that you are both on the same page, it also helps the feedback sink in. When the learner states that they agree with your feedback, you know they've absorbed it. If the learner disagrees or is confused by any of the feedback, discuss it until the individual is absolutely clear.

FINER POINTS OF COMMUNICATION

After you have focused on the big-picture communication issues, you must also consider the finer points of communication. With so many new communication technologies available to us, we sometimes don't use the right tool for the right job. What follows is a list of a few tools that will help you choose the best way to deliver your message.

Email

Email is overused and it can lead to miscommunication. Whenever possible, have a face-to-face discussion with someone to communicate an idea, a feeling, whatever. I love keeping a list of items I'd normally email to people at the company and then, at our weekly meeting, going through each item instead of wasting time sending the information via email.

Instant Messaging

I personally find instant messaging a complete pain and a distraction in day-to-day business except on one occasion: during conference calls. If I have two to three people on my side of a conference call, it's great to be able to send ideas back and forth to each other during the call. I've done calls with my lawyer listening in, and he and I would quickly ping each other with questions and suggestions about what to say or what not to say on the call. We tried using email, but we'd both end up being distracted by another random email instead; chatting via instant message was quicker and easier.

Video Chats

One of the best tools I've used in building companies recently has been video chat; I use both Skype and iChat. These are fantastic tools not only to keep in touch with people remotely but also to build relationships with them. I've found that if you can get a prospective client on a call using video chat it's much easier to build a relationship and close the deal. I also use video chat daily in coaching and mentoring entrepreneurs. If I had employees living and working remotely I would do all of our calls on video chat rather than over the phone. The connection is just so much stronger, and best of all, it's free!

New Media

I'm fine with Facebook, Twitter, and other new media. Gen Y uses them to connect, communicate, etc. So long as people hit their goals and get their work done, I don't care how they are communicating. It does make sense, however, for a company to say which form of written communication they prefer employees to use primarily. One rule that's worked well for me is actually based on an old legal principle called the Postal Acceptance Rule. Generally applied, it says that whatever form of communication is used to start a discussion is the form to use in continuing the discussion. So, if someone sends you a message on Facebook, you reply to them there, and if you prefer another venue, you ask them to continue the discussion using that medium from that point on.

—

When people come together in groups, communication becomes even more difficult. That is why it is so important that you prepare your organization for fast growth by carefully managing your meetings.

CHAPTER 6

FOCUSED MEETINGS

"A meeting is an event where minutes are taken and hours wasted."
—Captain James T. Kirk, *Star Trek*

If I put all of the people reading this book into a massive stadium and asked those present whether they've ever been in a boring meeting that dragged on forever, virtually every hand would go up. We've all been to one of those meetings where people say a lot and nothing seems to get resolved. However, this doesn't have to be the norm. In fact, if you want to take your business to the next level, it *shouldn't* be the norm.

As I mentioned before, meetings reflect the nature of your company's culture. If you want your culture to be energetic, focused, and accountable, your meetings have to embody those same characteristics. Your meetings can improve the atmosphere of your entire organization, or they can leave your company listless and without direction.

Getting to a place where your meetings mean something is a process, but I'll put you on the fast track with the following strategies. In addition, I'll outline the most effective types of meetings to implement in your organization. These two components will help you build a stronger company and a culture of energy, focus, and accountability.

FIVE STRATEGIES FOR TAKING BACK YOUR MEETINGS

Time and time again it's been shown that the optimal way to take and maintain control of company meetings large and small is to follow these five simple steps.

1. Prepare an agenda.

"No agenda, no attenda." I can't recall where I heard this phrase, but I've never forgotten it because it expresses exactly how I feel about meetings with no agenda—you shouldn't attend them. Meetings without clear agendas have a tendency to (1) go off track or (2) include individuals whose time would be better spent back at their desks, getting important projects completed.

Having an agenda also prevents the meeting from getting hijacked by a random topic. Publishing an agenda ahead of time allows introverted people in particular to prepare in advance what they'd like to share in the discussion. If they don't know the agenda ahead of time, most introverts will not respond at all in the allotted time but will leave the meeting full of their unspoken ideas.

An agenda also eliminates the need to start the meeting with someone saying, "Okay, so to lay out what we are going to do today . . ." Agendas save those otherwise wasted minutes of every meeting ever run.

Agendas can be short and sweet. In every invitation to a meeting include a bulleted list of action items so people can figure out what's going to be covered, and in what order.

Every successful meeting has a clear purpose, and it needs to be stated in one sentence and added to the meeting's agenda. Limit each meeting's possible outcomes to a maximum of three. This way, people will know why they have been asked to attend and what they will be expected to accomplish in the meeting.

If you want to, distribute a hard copy of the agenda to everyone at the beginning of the meeting. Again, this agenda will include the main purpose of the meeting, the possible outcomes, and the action items that are to be covered. I don't bother with hard copy handouts, but I do quickly read the agenda out loud so everyone remembers what we're covering. Assume that those attending the meeting have reviewed this material and go straight to the discussion of the action items.

2. Determine a meeting style.

There are basically three different styles of meetings: "information share," "creative discussion," and "consensus decision."

An information-share meeting consists of information flowing in one direction; either "up" to leadership from employees or "down" to employees from senior management. Requests for clarification can be entertained during this type of meeting, but there's no real debate or discussion.

Creative-discussion meetings revolve around the process of brainstorming and getting ideas out on the table without making any decisions about the feasibility or validity of what's produced. During this style of meeting, it's critical to have employees understand that at a later date key stakeholders will make decisions using the information collected.

When decisions need to be made, consensus-decision meetings should be held. These types of meetings tend to get pretty heated, and passionate feelings will almost certainly be expressed. Despite any conflicts that may arise, all participants must reach consensus. Once you've concluded the meeting, all feelings and conflicts should be left in the meeting room. Never continue the discussion outside of the meeting.

3. Start on time and end early.

When I lectured at MIT, I promised students we'd start on time. When I actually delivered on that promise, they were dumbfounded. If students weren't present at the start of class, or hadn't returned to the classroom after a break, we shut the door and started without them. Respect for people's time starts with a gesture as simple as that, but it helps you stay on course and remain mindful of the clock. For me it also reflects something much bigger. If you can't start a meeting on time, why would it be any different for anything else that's going on in a company? You couldn't produce goods or services on time. You couldn't deliver those goods and services on time. And so forth. There are exceptions, of course, but that's what they should be—exceptions.

Always end meetings five minutes *earlier* than scheduled. Why? This built-in five-minute buffer at the end of every meeting gives everyone time before their next meeting to grab a cup of coffee or water, go to the bathroom, chat with their assistant or coworkers, check a few emails, or simply to walk to the location of a meeting that might follow it. It's as simple as that.

Whenever possible, attempt to "compress time." When you are booking a meeting, book it for 50 percent of the time you first think you will need. For example, if you're scheduling a meeting you estimate will require one hour, book it and run it in thirty minutes instead. Like so many other obligations, meetings tend to fill the space you give them. By limiting the time for all meetings, you increase your productivity and implement a highly profitable system of time management.

4. Foster useful communication.

Ever notice how the same people tend to talk a lot in meetings and others never really speak up? In order to run successful meetings, you must engage every participant, especially the ones who typically remain silent, because they could really add value to the discussion. During meetings, foster dialogue with the newcomers or quiet folks first, and then go around the table, moving up in seniority as you solicit feedback or ideas. Leaders should always give feedback last so that they don't sway the group one way or the other.

Another strategy for fostering useful communication during longer creative-discussion meetings is to employ a strategy I learned from GE's WorkOut process. It's easy: simply give every meeting participant some adhesive notes and instruct them to write down five to ten ideas, one per note. I once did this with a client who wanted to find ways to increase revenue and decrease expenses. We gathered his forty employees in a room, and in only five minutes we'd generated 150 ideas, which were then put up on the wall as each person read his or her own ideas. Everyone contributed, even those who posted merely one or two comments. After the meeting, a few employees said it was the first time anyone had heard, listened to, or even asked for their ideas. Simple, and highly effective.

Yet another strategy that will help you foster communication in meetings is making sure people aren't distracted because they are responding to email on their mobile devices or laptops. I don't mind if people bring such portable devices to meetings—taking notes on your laptop is quite useful—but email distracts people from the task at hand. One easy way to fix this is to allow people to call each other out on covert emailing. Tell your employees that if they suspect someone is doing this, they can ask the person to stop typing and show everyone what he or she has been doing. If they catch colleagues emailing, the emailer owes $10 or $20 to the company's entertainment fund or a charity. Works like a charm. If an employee calls someone on it and are wrong, the accuser owes that person the money instead!

5. Know your role.

Every meeting should have a chair, a timekeeper, participants, and a closer. Let's go over the roles briefly.

The Chair

Any person chosen to chair a meeting identifies the type of meeting upon inviting participants, announces it again at the start of the meeting, and guides the meeting in keeping with the agenda. The chair also closes discussion five minutes before the end of the meeting to ensure that people can get to their next one. The job of the chair is to prevent a meeting from going sideways. If it is, the chair should stop it and correct the problem or suggest that the group rebook the meeting and try again later. The chair doesn't have to be the person who organized the meeting; he or she just has to be the person who will ensure that it runs smoothly.

The Timekeeper

This role is rather self-explanatory. Timekeepers make sure everyone stays on schedule and that all points in the agenda are covered. The timekeeper prevents the chair as well as the participants from lingering too long on any one point.

The Participants

Meeting attendees should not be passive observers. They need to arrive at meetings prepared to contribute and to remain interested throughout the meeting. Participants may also be responsible for maintenance of what I like to call the "Parking Lot." This is a repository for all ideas that may come up during the meeting but don't necessarily need to be handled during it. The issues stored in the Parking Lot can be addressed at a later date.

The Closer

As I mentioned earlier, the chair of any given meeting customarily acts as the closer. Meetings should always be closed with the chair posing this simple question: "Who's doing what, and by when?" Have each person in the meeting acknowledge what he or she is committed to doing and their deadline for doing it. By closing meetings in this way, you ensure that people don't start projects based on items that were merely being discussed in the meeting. You also make it nearly impossible for people to leave the meeting without outlining their next steps.

After the chair has closed the meeting, the senior leader present needs to determine whether another meeting is necessary, when it should be held, and whether any other participants should be present.

TYPES OF MEETINGS YOU NEED TO IMPLEMENT NOW

Now that you have practical strategies for how to conduct meetings and the roles to choose from, you need to know what types of meetings you need to implement, and why. In this section, I'll outline all of the meetings that I think, ideally, belong in any business.

One thing to remember is that meetings can't be effective if there's no system in place to ensure their regular occurrence. You need a series of different meetings to achieve various objectives, and these meetings need to happen even when you or other members of the team are not able to attend. When you get into a rhythm with these meetings, you'll wonder how you ever got things done before you established them.

Retreats: Yearly/Quarterly

Both yearly and quarterly retreats are critical for leadership and business teams to ensure alignment, team building, and productive engagement. Yearly retreats should be done in about two days; quarterly retreats can be fit into just one day. I'm a firm believer that retreats should be done off-site, if possible, and in an environment where group interaction is feasible. There's just something that changes when a team is removed from its usual environment, such as the city, and relocated to a cabin or a chalet away from distractions like bars and restaurants. The goal here is to learn, work, and live together. I find that the more rustic the location, the tighter the bond created with the team. I also love having retreats where there's some kind of active rest in which everyone can participate together, even if it's just going for long hikes in the mountains or around a lake.

Once you've found a place in which to engage on a much deeper level, the main work to be done during a retreat is prioritizing yearly or quarterly objectives. It always works best to review the Painted Picture right at the start of the first day. When everyone systematically reads the Painted Picture each quarter, the decision making becomes a lot tighter and more focused on high-impact projects rather than the big shiny objectives that can easily distract companies. Allowing two days for yearly retreats yields serious discussion and debate about projects, time during which the group digs into the root cause of any uncertainty and ensures that the right projects have, indeed, been chosen.

Board of Advisers Meeting: Quarterly

I will discuss this type of meeting in detail in chapter 13. At this point, just remember that your quarterly board of advisers meeting should include a review of your Painted Picture, a review of your financials, and a discussion of your company's future. This is the meeting where you discuss how you will achieve the growth you desire.

Business Area Review: Quarterly

A "Business Area Review," or BAR, is a quarterly meeting we used at the height of some rapid growth in a company I was building in the late nineties. This type of meeting produces an amazing culture of accountability. Every quarter, each business area would present the following:

- What was accomplished during the prior quarter
- Quarterly metrics and an explanation of them
- A plan to drive metrics and get projects accomplished in the upcoming quarter

Everyone presented in front of the executive leadership of the company and the heads of all the other business areas. This meant the BAR was like a peer review. It was a high-pressure meeting, but in a good way. The process of having employees present in front of the leadership team also created leaders within the company. I've seen this work fantastically well with business areas presenting to the board of advisers too.

Profit Sharing: Monthly

Every month, we had a program called the Great Game of Business, or GGOB for short, which was based on the book by the same name written by Jack Stack.

Sharing a percentage of a company's profits with employees is great, but employees have to earn it and treat profits the same way owners do. How? Once a month, get all the employees to meet and review the company's income statement together. Look for and obsess as a team about how to make more money and how to save money on the business. I learned this process twenty years ago running a painting business. I'd hired nine of my friends, and they all hated me because I seemed to be making all the money. The reality was that I hadn't even *started* making money yet! They knew what my revenues were, but they had no idea what my expenses were, and that meant they all thought I was making more profit than I was. So, when I started to show them that I wasn't making any money, they got scared for me, they got scared for themselves, and thought, "Hell, if we don't get this guy to grow a little bit more and help him save more money and be profitable, we might be out of a job partway through our year."

If you're running a wildly successful and profitable business, there's no sense trying to hide it. I talked to a business owner from Las Vegas once who was nervous about letting his employees know how much money he was making. "Dude," I said, "they know you're rich! There's a forty-foot limo outside waiting for you, not to mention your two private jets. *They get it!*"

Give employees a percentage of the profits and watch how much more money you'll start to make.

Here are the overall best tips for running a successful profit-sharing meeting.

- Make the meetings monthly.
- For employees to earn profit sharing, they must attend every monthly meeting unless they are on vacation or out of town on business.
- Hand out copies of the profit and loss statement at the start of the meeting and then collect and shred the copies after the meeting.
- Assign one person from any business area to be accountable for reviewing a specific expense for a different business area and reporting waste at the monthly meeting. The person reports on one line item only: for example, someone in marketing might report for three to six months on telephone expenses for the whole company; someone in IT might dig into and report on travel.
- At each meeting teach employees one to three new things about finance: for example, go over definitions of terms (margin, EBIT, etc.), show them ratios, show them a balance sheet, and so on.
- Consider distributing part of the profits or bonuses two to three times a year.

"WAR" Meetings: Weekly

Teams need a weekly meeting structure to update each other and stay on the same page. One simple meeting that's worked for me since the mid-nineties is called a "Weekly Action Review," or WAR. It's a weekly ninety-minute meeting that each business area holds for its entire team. The format is based on a process called "Forum Meetings" used by Entrepreneurs' Organization and Young Presidents' Organization.

The first thirty minutes of WAR requires that each person give a quick three- to five-minute update that answers these questions:

- What went well last week?
- What didn't go well last week?
- Where am I stuck?
- What are the top three things I'll be working on this week?

Simply by following this system, every person on any given team stays aligned with what that team is working on each week.

As part of the second thirty minutes, the team reviews the metrics on the dashboard for that business area, looking for areas of concern as well as bright spots. By reviewing the key numbers for their business area every week, people start holding each other accountable, and they realize that because their key metrics roll up to the leadership team's attention, they need to figure out the answers before they are asked.

During the final thirty minutes of WAR, the group tries to "un-stick" some of the areas that team members were stuck on earlier. The group works together to share experiences and ideas to help out their teammates. This simple sharing process is really influential in building a team, as opposed to allowing the creation of silos, which prevent unification.

As your company grows in the number of employees it's hired, your leadership team will have its WAR meeting, and then ideally, right afterward, each business area will have its own WAR. In this way members of the leadership team can sit in on business area WARs to either participate or just be a fly on the wall.

Strategy Meetings: Weekly

Weekly or even semimonthly meetings with leadership to talk about opportunities that are three to six months out really build a strong strategic mindset within the company. This type of meeting also assures that the team has time to handle this area of the business, which often gets overlooked due to the urgency of the day-to-day.

Goal Setting and Review: Weekly

Goal Setting and Review, GS&R for short, is perhaps the most consequential type of meeting I've learned about thus far. Over the years I've learned more and more about how to make this meeting highly effective. I've included a sample GS&R format in appendix 2, and I have also included one on my website (www.BackPocketCOO.com).

So, just what *is* GS&R? It's essentially a one-on-one meeting that you have with each person who reports directly to you. During GS&R, you set goals with your direct reports for the upcoming week and align their goals with the objectives of your team and the company. I've even used this meeting very successfully in coaching franchisees.

GS&R is meant to be a blend of direction, development, and support—it's *not* an opportunity for task or project follow-up. *Direction* helps ensure that what people were working on was relevant and focused on the critical needs of the company. *Development* assesses the employee's skill development in the areas they need to know and keep learning. The *support* component addresses the need for emotional support for the employee—it's tough to be in certain jobs, especially in high-growth environments. The simple weekly meeting plan provided rhythm and a ton of focus for all of us.

Fortune magazine asked me once, "How do you motivate your employees?" I said: "I don't. I refuse to try to motivate people. What I want to do is try to take people who are already motivated and inspire them to do the stuff they know they have to do, and give them the systems and tools to create change. Then be there to support them." You shouldn't be in the business of motivating people. But helping align and focus people who are *already* motivated is a recipe for your company's growth.

I like to have weekly GS&Rs for thirty to sixty minutes. During these meetings you coach your team one-on-one, demonstrating how to be more effective in their roles. It's also where I practice "situational leadership," an idea developed by Ken Blanchard and Paul Hersey. Done right, this meeting should eliminate 80 percent of the emails between you and your direct reports during the week. How? Instead of emailing each other with random questions and ideas, you add those to a list to be discussed at the Monday GS&R, saving you both tons of time during the week. Needless to say, it also saves a lot of frustration caused by the miscommunication that frequently occurs over email.

Huddle: Daily

If I had to name one meeting we used at 1-800-GOT-JUNK? that had the most powerful impact on our whole team, this might have been it. The "Huddle" is a concept we learned from Verne Harnish at Gazelles, based on his Rockefeller Habits program. Ours was a seven-minute, all-company, stand-up meeting that started precisely at 10:55 and ended at 11:02. We ran it every day for years, and they still run it at 1-800-GOT-JUNK? to this day.

I'm going to be honest here because you need to be prepared. When we first started the Huddle, it was awkward, and people hated it. We kept at it, however, and after weeks of "fake it 'til you make it" and trying a number of versions, it started to work. We'd debrief behind the scenes a couple of times a week to discuss what we could do to make it better. We even phoned other companies to learn about what they were doing to make Huddle a success. And as we grew, Huddle had to change in order to work with more and more employees.

Here's the format for a successful Huddle, shaped by that trial-and-error period.

Good News. The first couple of minutes, anyone can share good news or praise other business areas, work with customers, fellow employees, and so forth. This good news really should be related to the company or what employees in the company have done.

Numbers. Review and post the key metrics from your sales funnel so everyone has a window into the key numbers for the business. Ideally, three to five metrics can be posted daily with indicators as to whether those numbers are above or below forecast. If Rockefeller looked at the numbers daily from his oil fields in Russia using the world's first telex, why wouldn't we share the key numbers with our employees?

What Does It All Mean? We did a daily forecast on the monthly (and yearly) revenue versus budget. It was awesome to show the team how we were doing on a daily basis instead of waiting until the end of the month to add it all up.

Departmental Update. With roughly eight business areas in the company, we rotated and had one business area update the entire company. They'd start by bringing us up to date on how their business area was doing with their top three items for the quarter (for more on the top-three system, see page 182). Then they'd let us know everything else they were working on that coming week. It was an amazing glimpse into each business area. It was also a way to systematically guarantee that business areas were always focused on their quarterly top three projects.

Missing Systems/Frustrations. We'd then share any missing systems we'd found or things that were frustrating us in some area of the business. Anyone could share these, and it was always done in a no-blame environment. After each frustration was shared, someone else would raise their hand and simply say "I'll take it," meaning they would take ownership and see to it that the problem got fixed. No debate or discussion happened during a Huddle: issues were simply raised and then someone offered to resolve them.

Cheer. We'd then finish Huddle with what we called the "High Gloss Cheer," named after Christopher "High Gloss" Bennett, who was always a huge culture booster for the company. The cheer was something based on the good news we'd heard that day at Huddle. And yes, it was dorky at first, but everyone grew to love it, and it always ended Huddle on a high note.

Adrenaline: Daily

As 1-800-GOT-JUNK? grew from sixteen people at Huddle to eventually more than 120 attending, at times, a few business areas wanted to get more of a pulse for their respective areas. They put in place a short three-minute pre-Huddle meeting called "Adrenaline." It was a fast-paced update where each person on the team would say what he or she was working on that day. It was a great way to be able to quickly add ideas or take note of something you would grab someone later to chat about.

Debrief Meetings: Ad Hoc

These quick five- to ten-minute meetings allow a team that ran a project, event, or call to debrief others on how it went. They are always less formal and booked on an ad hoc basis. This type of meeting helps to uncover areas that went well, were very effective, or didn't work at all and should be avoided or done differently next time. Just slowing down to have these quick meetings will help you go faster next time. I've always made it a habit to meet with teams after these types of occurrences to quickly share ideas while they were fresh in our minds.

—

This may seem like a lot of meetings. And it is. However, it's having these meetings, and running all meetings using these highly effective tools, that will allow your company to run faster. They will help reduce email, further reducing the risk of miscommunication. Employee frustration will drop drastically. And your team won't be wasting time in the useless types of meetings that are held in businesses today. With time and effort, all of these meetings can be used in your company to help get more done, with fewer people, faster.

CHAPTER 7

FOCUSED MARKETING

"A market is never saturated with a good product, but it is very quickly saturated with a bad one."
—Henry Ford

In all my years of building companies, my marketing efforts have been based on focus rather than specific marketing tactics. Before you read this chapter, review your Painted Picture to see what you want your marketing to deliver in three years. This chapter will show you how you can realize that vision and get on the track to doubling the size of your business.

While I won't offer you any silver bullets that magically market your product or service, I promise you'll be able to find practical ways of marketing that won't break the bank. They're all simple solutions that will keep your brand top of mind in your target market and turn prospects into paying clients.

My first marketing experiences were with College Pro Painters in Sudbury, Ontario. At twenty-one years of age, I was given a franchise territory of about ninety thousand people, and I was enthusiastic about being able to market house painting services to *all* of them! The truth was, I didn't need to market to every single person in my territory. In order to make a profit, I only needed to paint 150 out of the 35,000 houses in Sudbury. I learned my first lesson in marketing: it's less about marketing to everyone and more about marketing to those most likely to have a need for your services. I had to get my name in front of the people who were most likely to buy. In short, the name of the marketing game was *focus*.

FOCUS

At College Pro Painters, we knew that the type of clients we wanted lived on curvy streets and that their houses had brass kick plates on the front doors. Our prospective clients had manicured lawns and drove BMWs and Volvos. And, most importantly, their houses were in need of a paint job but weren't completely falling apart. Once I knew which group to focus on, I marketed solely to them rather than the entire city of Sudbury. Some neighborhoods were completely ignored while others were targeted every week all summer long.

My marketing efforts were so focused that if prospects called from areas outside of my target market, I simply told them I didn't service their areas. Some might balk at turning away a customer, but I was focused on building my name in *my* target market. I was willing to walk away from clients who were outside of my focus areas rather than risk having other prospects within my target areas wanting to hire me and being unable to. Losing my focus would spread my resources too thin. While this may seem counterintuitive, you'll see that it's not if you look at it from a brand-building perspective: rather than being just another company of professional painters, College Pro Painters was being molded into the painting company of choice for a very specific market, and I was counting on the profitability that comes from being so hyper-focused.

A few years later, I proved that the concept of focused marketing to targeted prospects really worked. Still with College Pro Painters, I hired a franchisee named Rob Gallagher, whom I trained and mentored. Rob owned an area called Chapin Estates, with a population of 1,667 people. Although there were roughly six hundred homes in his area, Rob needed to paint just thirty of those houses to make a killing that summer. I showed him that, on average, people painted their homes every five years, which meant that approximately 120 houses would need to be painted that summer. We put a plan in place so that every one of those 120 houses knew the name "College Pro Painters." Rob told me later that summer that people called him by name in the neighborhood because he'd gotten in front of them so many times. Rob saw that a 25 percent market share was possible because he was going to be more focused than all the competitors. He ended up painting forty houses that summer and made $20,000 in profit. Not bad for a twenty-year-old university student in 1989.

People won't think to use your product or service if they don't know your brand. They also won't think to use your product or service if they're not inclined to do so in the first place. Your job? Find the *right* audience and get the *right* message out there. Your efforts to raise recognition of your brand don't have to be complicated, either. Before you begin, however, think about what brand(s) you want to draw attention to. Are you marketing a specific product, product line, your company name, etc.? You may have multiple products or services; in that case, you'll want to have a strategy in place for each of them.

Once you've determined your target market, you need to focus on providing the widest possible exposure for your brand. Here are some easy ways to start getting your name out there.

BOOTSTRAP ADVERTISING

My grandparents were cheap—they were Scottish, so they can blame their heritage—and they taught me to "make do" and "reuse" far before it was trendy to do so. I learned from them at an early age how to bootstrap, and that "be cheap" mentality carried over to my marketing, and still does. In every aspect of your marketing campaign, you should make every penny count.

Paying for advertising just seems wrong. It seems like too much of a risk. And until I've tried everything else that I *know* will work, I just won't take the chance on marketing that *might* work.

Want to learn how you can pitch stories and articles to get free media coverage? What follows are a few tips I've gleaned from my experiences that will help you get the most value from your advertising efforts—and from your dollars when you do have to spend them.

Barter.

One of the biggest and best-kept secrets ever is that *every* magazine, newspaper, website, and TV or radio station will barter for their advertising space.

All of these types of advertising outlets have no hard costs for running ads. For TV and radio, it's airtime. For magazines and newspapers, it's a piece of paper they have to print whether they've sold all the ads that can fit on it or not. Often, and especially now, magazines will run ads for free or very cheaply if they are going to print the next day. Once Tuesday's edition goes to press, it's over for that specific window of sales potential. It's not as if it were a bottle of wine they could sell tomorrow if they didn't sell it today. All media outlets have expiring inventory, and they will sell their space for whatever price they can negotiate.

Years ago, I ran a very large barter company, and we had tons of clients in advertising. They would all trade advertising space for products from other companies. All those ads you see in magazines for golf courses and hotels were not paid for with cash. They were all paid for by the golf course trading twenty, fifty, or one hundred green fees in exchange for the ad, or the hotel agreeing to ten to twenty nights in a luxury room or suite for the ad. It doesn't cost a golf course anything to trade green fees except the cost of a scorecard and pencil—the golf course will still be there the next day to resell to someone paying cash. The same is true for the hotel. If you can trade your products or services with the media, they'll turn around and resell it for cash to their clients later.

Even bloggers will trade space for something they want. The key is for you to find something *you* have that is of value to them. Give them some of your products or services in exchange for an equal or greater amount of credit, gift certificates, and so on. That will save cash and get you marketing exposure for your brand.

Negotiate.

If you can't barter, don't be afraid to negotiate the price; all advertising gets cheaper the closer it is to the date or time the ad will run. I've negotiated millions of dollars of radio and TV ads that were "preemptable." We got them for 50 percent off, but if someone else came along willing to pay full price, the station would cancel our ads. "Great," I'd say. "I'm building a brand for years to come. I'll take as many 50 percent-off ads as I can get." Let your competitors pay full price.

Bootstrapping also carries over into producing your marketing materials. There are plenty of websites around, like CrowdSpring (at www.crowdspring.com), where dozens of people will produce creative work for you, yet you pay only the person whose work you love best, a process called crowdsourcing. You can also use old-fashioned outsourcing using great sites like www.Guru.com or www.eLance.com to develop everything from your company logo to ad layouts to glossy marketing brochures.

I've learned to produce marketing materials inexpensively in other ways as well. I hired actors, but instead of paying them to model for a photo shoot, I gave them a quarter load of junk removal free of charge. When we were just starting out, we hired a good-looking young guy who fit our brand for $200 cash for unlimited use of his photo. It ended up being on hundreds of thousands of marketing pieces—the equivalent of $5,000 in actor's fees. I've even made TV ads in which every actor we used was a friend of the company, and they all offered their time and talent for no money.

I have clients in Berlin who refused to pay a fixed price for commercials and convinced the TV station that if the ads were "really going to work," the TV station could share in the risk and the potential gains. They are buying discounted TV advertising and paying the station a percentage of the revenues it generates.

Be unconventional.

In today's ad-choked media environment, sometimes simpler, more direct marketing efforts yield the best results. Let me share with you a few inexpensive marketing ideas that I have found to be effective in generating a brand buzz.

Corporate Clothing.

You've got to wear clothes, so why not put them to work marketing your product or service? It's an easy win for your company, and in some instances, such as at networking events and conferences, corporate clothing will help you stand out in a sea of suits. For example, at one conference that had roughly two thousand attendees, the four of us from 1-800-GOT-JUNK? each wore a shirt with a huge corporate logo on the back. We really stood out, so much so, in fact, that many people thought there were at least twenty of us walking around because they saw our logos so often amid the masses of suit jackets. At SXSW, start-up companies have even been known to pay people to wear their T-shirts and walk around the venue, which builds a brand army instantly.

Every time I wear branded clothing, someone comments and asks me about my company. Even as far back as College Pro Painters, our painters wore shirts emblazoned with our logo so that while they were up on ladders people would see our brand. This also proves helpful when recruiting new employees. For instance, one summer I had my painters wear their company shirt to the university pub. I bribed them with free beer to do it, and needless to say, it helped me find new painters every time.

While building 1-800-GOT-JUNK?, I would place my branded jacket on the outside of chairs so it would be seen while I was sitting down. On planes, I'd fold it in such a way that the logo stood out even when placed in overhead bins. I was relentlessly getting my name out to prospects. I even had custom license plates made with my company name on them for two companies I built.

"Parketing"

I can't recall who gave it this name, but "parketing," or the practice of parking branded vehicles at high-traffic locations, has been around forever. My dad used to have his company logos and lists of the products he sold painted onto our family station wagon! It served as a rolling billboard, and he always parked it strategically: no matter where we went, he found the spot that would garner the most views from passing pedestrians and other drivers.

At College Pro Painters, many of us painted our old, used vehicles bright yellow and decorated them with our red and white company logo. These "Big Bird" vans, as they were called, attracted attention and got us clients. Some franchisees even bartered with gas station owners: in exchange for parking their vans at the stations overnight, College Pro Painters would buy gas from the proprietor all summer long. The arrangement benefited all those involved and put College Pro Painters front and center at all times of the day.

This method can be used in any company where corporate vehicles are used. We implemented the parketing method at 1-800-GOT-JUNK? and met with the same success, and we also made sure that our logo-laden trucks were parked some place highly visible at night. Even potential repair costs due to vandalism are far outweighed by the free marketing exposure you'll get.

"27 Hits"

You truly *see* only one out of every three ads put in front of you. And you take action only after you've *seen* a brand's marketing nine times. So, it takes something like "27 hits" from a brand before a prospect even responds. Think about that for a second. Are your prospective customers getting all 27 hits?

Twenty years ago, I was recruiting College Pro Painters franchisees at Queen's University, and I decided to hammer them with 27 hits in forty-eight hours to really drive as much awareness of the company as possible and get potential candidates in the door fast. So, five of us hit the campus like a tidal wave: we parked our Big Bird van near the student union; we placed over one hundred lawn signs around campus; we handed out flyers at meal lines in the cafeterias; we put the same flyers under doors in dorms. (Sometimes we were asked to leave, which to us meant, "Leave this floor and go to the next one.") While we did all this, we were each wearing a huge College Pro Painters logo on our winter coat, of course.

The onslaught continued the next day. We went into classrooms and put flyers on desks and chairs, and we set up tables in the main buildings where we'd hand out flyers to students. We even telephoned each student who lived on campus and whose parents' home address was in cities where we needed franchisees. At the end of two days, there wasn't anyone we cared about who didn't know we wanted franchisees. We easily hit our marketing goals with these guerrilla-marketing efforts. What did our competitors do? They ran an ad in the paper.

Handwritten Notes

As I mentioned in the beginning of the chapter, grandparents are chock full of wisdom, so when you're thinking about running your business, think about the simplicity of their rules and make sure they're incorporated into the way you run your business.

Simple, handwritten thank-you notes go miles. I actually had a bit of a spat with my wife about this the other day because I thought she should write notes to people to say thank you (I could get my lazy butt doing it, too, but that's not the point). Her response was that she calls or emails people to say thanks, and I said that it's just not the same. *Nothing* beats a handwritten thank-you note. It's even more powerful today in our electronic world of fleeting, detached encounters. Getting a handwritten note means you took the time to show your gratitude the *right* way. And they don't have to be ones with company logos on them or anything special. As grandmas always say, it's the thought that counts.

Jack Daly, internationally renowned professional sales coach and speaker, takes the handwritten thank-you note philosophy one step further. Jack takes photos of himself with people, often in fun situations. He then uploads those photos to Shutterfly.com, SendOutCards.com, or a similar website where he can quickly type up a personal note to accompany the card. Then, *presto*, the service mails the card to the person's address for Jack, and his account gets billed. And yeah, you guessed it—those cards don't get thrown away. Instead, they stay as little marketing reminders to his friends. (Note: Regardless of who you are, send me a card with a photo of you holding my book. That would be awesome.)

FOCUSED MARKETING ON A DAILY BASIS

I began this chapter by describing the importance of defining the right target audience for your products and services. I'm ending it with a real-life example of just how successful the right type of focused marketing—that is, marketing directed toward the target audience you identified for your company—can be.

In the early days at 1-800-GOT-JUNK?, we had a franchisee who was struggling. They just weren't getting enough work to cover their costs.

We knew that it was more about their team making a focused effort than it was about their territory not being lucrative enough. We knew it was about doing more of the *right* things and less about having some new, perfectly designed flyer.

So, what did we do to help them do the *right* things to increase their business? We set up a program called KAMP: Kick Ass Marketing Program. We gave them a list of marketing tasks they had to do every single day, and at the end of each day, they reported in to us, letting us know what they had accomplished. Each and every day for a couple of months they documented all of the marketing they did. We'd get an email back from them with rough notes like: "500 Post-it notes on cars at the grocery store; 25 signs up on poles; 7 signs up on client's lawns; 4 cold calls to property managers." And each day after reading what they'd done, we would quickly hammer another email out to them guiding them on what marketing to do the next day and where specifically to do it.

KAMP was successful because I'd been so successful as a franchisee with College Pro Painters. Focused marketing was how I was able to sign up so many great franchisees with Boyd Autobody, and it was how our 1-800-GOT-JUNK? Franchise Partners were going to be successful, too. It was about *focus*. In the early days, 1-800-GOT-JUNK? had just five marketing pieces. Years later, we had about 120 different marketing pieces. Yet I'm convinced to this day that we could have been just as successful with only the five we started with.

In fact, forty years after College Pro Painters started, I'll bet they still don't have any more than five to seven marketing pieces, but they do work for more than fifty thousand customers each summer. It's about *focus*, not tactics.

CHAPTER 8

FOCUSED PUBLIC RELATIONS

*"Next to doing the right thing, the most important thing is
to let people know you are doing the right thing."*
—John D. Rockefeller

If you're looking for a better way to land free coverage for your product or service online, in newspapers and magazines, or on radio and TV, keep reading. The practices I describe in this chapter have helped me land free PR for more than twenty-two years, and I've taught thousands of companies to do the same. At one point, as a matter of fact, I built and led a team that generated more than 5,200 media hits for one company over a six-year period. That coverage included mentions on *The Oprah Winfrey Show, Dr. Phil, The Big Idea with Donny Deutsch,* CNN, CNBC, and in *Fortune,* the *Wall Street Journal, New York Times,* and virtually every other major newspaper and business periodical in the United States.

In this chapter I'll share with you how my team came to generate that spectacular media coverage. I'd like to begin, however, by making the crucial distinction between PR and marketing to save you from wasting resources as you bark up the wrong tree.

PR IS *NOT* MARKETING

Marketing and communications are very different from PR, but people often substitute one for the other. Big mistake. PR, in the way that I've been doing it in my career, is a *sales role,* and you need to treat it like a *sales function*. Typically, marketing or communications people are not wired the same way as salespeople are. It takes a salesperson to make PR work.

To double the size of your company, you will have to double the PR exposure of your brand. You may not be able to get on *Oprah*, but the right PR strategies will get you a long way.

YOU'RE DOING THE MEDIA A FAVOR

Part of my plan for securing free PR means talking about my ideas to the content producers for magazines, websites, and television programs. Why would they want to listen? Simple: because great content means it's easier to sell ads, and ad sales mean profit. And, in general, editors don't generate content.

How do media outlets make money? How does a newspaper or magazine make money?

They make money by selling advertising.

What helps the magazine or newspaper sell advertising?

Having lots of readers.

And companies will purchase advertising with different media outlets that have lots of readers or viewers or impressions. Magazines are the perfect example: they don't make much money off of circulation. They make all of their profit by selling advertising, and the only way they sell advertising is by having really, really good content. Having outstanding content guarantees that readers want to buy those magazines.

"The harder I work, the luckier I get."

This quotation applies to everyone who is about to embark on a mission to generate free PR. The system only works if *you* work hard at implementing it, and this takes time.

If PR is a sales function, then you are in the business of selling ideas to media outlets. Selling anything is tough, but the advantage you have is that you are selling these ideas at no charge. The media outlets like things that are free, especially when it could lead to profit on their end. However, no one likes freebies that come with a really long instruction manual, which is why writers don't like getting press releases or difficult assignments. Writers love being inspired and writing their own stories. With the system I'm about to describe, you will be able to sell writers and journalists a couple of little idea snippets and then let them fill in the blanks on their own. In addition to writers, photographers and other media professionals are always looking for the next great cover shot. Give them one.

So remember: when you give the media free content, you're not only gaining exposure for your business but also making it possible for them to make their publications or stations better. You're helping them make money, and you're helping their staff look good too. Everybody wins.

WHERE TO PLACE YOUR STORY

When you start to think about where to sell your story, you need to focus your efforts on the media outlets that will give you the greatest direct benefits. To sharpen your focus, ask yourself these questions:

- Where would you like to be covered?
- What trade journals do your clients read?
- What media outlets would give maximum exposure to your products, services, or corporate culture?
- Why are you trying to land PR?

Once you know the answers to those questions, you're ready to start mapping out your PR strategy.

First, make a list of all the media outlets you want to cover your company. Think about TV, radio, online, magazines, newspapers, e-zines, blogs, newsletters, trade journals, and community papers. Ask your employees for ideas as well. They may know about interesting media outlets that you have never heard of.

Send some simple surveys out to all your customers and potential customers using free tools like SurveyMonkey (www.SurveyMonkey.com). Ask them what trade magazines they read and what media outlets they watch or listen to daily and weekly, and then target the ones most closely related to your business angle.

Go online and grab free lists of the top newspapers and magazines by circulation, top blogs by readers, and so forth. Once you have those lists, have your team pick five from each category. Stay hyper-focused. Resist the urge to simply say they'd all be good. It shouldn't take you more than an hour to do this whole exercise, and the focus it provides will be extremely beneficial.

Next, focus on the individuals who produce stories for those media outlets. Who covers your industry? Who covers your competitors? Who has covered similar companies in other industries? All of those people can write about you, too.

The key is to find the best writers and journalists within each of those media outlets. Remember, someone who covers oil and gas companies won't write about a medical supply company. Someone who covers mergers and acquisitions won't write about your company's corporate culture.

Likewise, remind your staff not to focus on contacting editors. Editors are the kings and queens of "no." They are not the ones who are in the business of digging up new ideas. They are in the business of editing every approved idea and rejecting most of the others. So focus on contacting writers and producers, not editors.

Contact information for writers, journalists, and photographers can be obtained through services like PR Newswire's MEDIAtlas or CisionPoint's Media Database. You can also find contact information quickly by entering the person's name, company, and the word "phone" or "address" into an online search engine. In a worst-case scenario, you can always call the main switchboard and ask for the person by name. Hint: I always do this in a tone of voice that implies that the person is practically my lifelong friend. I just casually say, "Oh hi, Mike Smith, please," and if the receptionist asks if I'd like his voicemail I say, "Sure; what's his direct line again so I don't bother you next time?" It usually works.

Here are a couple more tips. Whenever you have a great interview with a writer, ask what other publications he or she works for. One writer I asked years ago wrote pieces for a crummy little trade journal—and *Entrepreneur* (bingo!). And when you have your photo taken for a story, ask the photographer what other publications he or she shoots for, since this person may be able to introduce you to writers too.

More Resources

Besides PR Newswire (which used to cost approximately $1,500 per year but is rumored to be dropping its prices) and CisionPoint, Help a Reporter Out (HARO) is another great resource for getting in touch with the media, and it's free. This service, like PR Newswire, allows journalists to send out requests for experts, and if you fit the criteria, you can simply respond to their request via email. It's an easy way to land additional free press. Treat these freelancers and journalists well because they're always looking for experts for future stories.

Another great resource if you're going to do PR in-house rather than hire a PR firm or consultant is to purchase the modules from "PR in a Box" at www.PRInABox.ca.

I'm not a big fan of monitoring the coverage you generate except by using Google Alerts, which is free. If for some reason you want to waste the time and money tracking the fruits of your labor, then you can use the following services, but I'd just rather pour that time into landing more PR:

- Cision MediaSource Monitoring
- PR Newswire eWatch
- Burrelles*Luce*

CRAFTING YOUR PR SALES PITCHES

Once you've identified where you want to place your story, you have to make sure you have your angle and your pitch ready to deliver. I've outlined three easy steps to help you craft your PR sales pitches in order to greatly increase your percentage of wins. (Go to my website, www.BackPocketCOO.com, for more details on the system I'm about to describe.)

1. Know your angle.

The two basic questions you must ask yourself in order to determine your angle are "What is my story idea?" and "What will I pitch to the writer I'm about to contact?"

When you were starting your business and trying to pitch it to your spouse, your banker, or your parents (to get money or simply to explain why you were starting this business), you probably told them a story about how your great idea came about. Those stories—whatever you were saying to convince them your idea was a great one—consisted of three or four angles. Those are the three or four things that the media could write about.

- "I'm going to be successful because I'm a female entrepreneur."
- "I'm married and I run this company with my spouse."
- "I'm going to become successful because I quit my job to do this."
- "I dropped out of school to pursue this business idea."

Any of those explanations is a potential story. When you read through newspapers and magazines from now on, be certain to read with two different lenses: one that reads for enjoyment, and one that identifies the angles that reporters and writers use to create stories. By engaging yourself in this way, you'll start to see potential angles everywhere.

Potential angles could include story ideas related to

- Your sales approach or strategy
- Your advertising and marketing methods
- The systems you use to run your business
- Your product or service's features
- The importance of IT in running your business
- Your personal entrepreneur story
- Lessons from the edge when you almost lost your company
- Charity projects or efforts to give back to your community
- Stories about how you created your signature corporate culture
- Strategic alliances you've established
- Stories about specific employees

I encourage you to go to my website (www.BackPocketCOO.com) for a worksheet to help you craft your angles. Remember, when you're creating angles, think about the media piece from the perspective of the viewer or reader. Why will the audience care? What would the audience find important, intriguing, funny, etc.? Read five or six issues of the magazine you want to be covered in to learn how the writers write, so you can match your angles to it. Watch the TV show you want to be on repeatedly so you can learn how they like to title the episodes, and your angles will start to match their style.

Write each bullet succinctly, clearly, and in commonly used language so you can literally read a list of them from the page while talking to a reporter.

Pretend you are reading a story about each angle: have you listed all the bullet points that you want the audience to know and be captivated by?

Ensure that each of the bullets is as compelling as possible and could actually get a reader to forward the story to a friend.

2. Know your audience.

Every media outlet targets a different type of reader or viewer. When you're pitching your stories to writers, keep their audience in mind and ask yourself these questions:

- Why will their audience care?
- Why will my story help their audience purchase the magazine or tell others about the show they watched?

Here are examples of well-known media outlets and the audiences each one targets.

Bloomberg typically covers financial information, and discusses publicly traded companies. If you're pitching Bloomberg, make sure you're not a privately held company.

Oprah typically has emotional, heartrending stories. Don't try to sell her producers anything but stories that fit this description.

Forbes typically covers bigger businesses like Apple and Starbucks. You might want to rethink trying to sell a reporter on covering your small business.

Inc. covers start-ups. If you have a small business, consider this the ideal medium to pitch stories to about why yours is unique.

Even on a local level, different newspapers may lean further to the left or right in their coverage. Be aware of that before you pitch a story about your business to anyone who works at these publications.

3. Pick up the phone.

My most successful pitches to the media have come from using the good old telephone—*not* by sending an email. (Everyone asks me about email pitches, by the way. Sorry, that's not my gig. Everyone is writing about how to email members of the media, but I'm all about picking up the phone. I like competing where there is no competitor!)

Writers wake up every day, go to their offices, sit down at their desks, stare at their computers, and think, "What the hell am I going to write about today?"

They're not looking at their email. They're trying to get inspired to write about something.

When the phone rings, they'll answer it.

Now, when editors go to their offices, they sit with a stack of press releases in front of them. Those press releases came in over the newswire, as emails, and via fax machines, and guess what the editor does for the first two hours every day? He or she rejects almost all of those press releases.

Given a choice, would you call the editor who says no all day or the writer who is just waiting for inspiration? You call the writer, of course!

That's why I've always treated PR like a sales role: it involves picking up the phone and *selling* the content producer, the writer, on taking your story.

PREPPING FOR THE PITCH

When you're pitching your content to the writer, you should have at least two to three potential angles to sell. That way, if the person doesn't like the first angle, or you can't make that first angle fit the medium's particular needs, you can sell the writer on a second story angle while you've got him/her on the phone.

Prior to pitching the story, you need to do this basic prep:

1. Come up with a catchy title like, "An Entrepreneurial Resource You Keep in Your Back Pocket." Exercise caution, though. You're not writing the actual title *for* the writer; you're coming up with a headline that's creative and compelling enough to catch the writer's

attention so you can pitch your angle about the story you want him or her to write.

2. For each angle or title, you need to list four to five key bullets to help the writer craft a story. Some examples that correspond to the sample title I used in item one include:

    • Entrepreneurs and their teams have scheduled access to Cameron Herold monthly.
    • They get access to his skills at one-tenth the cost of hiring someone with his skills full-time.
    • They get access to him whenever they need him for a quick call or email. Just like having him in their back pocket.

3. Now list five key bullets about your company that you will mention to the media *every time you interact*, regardless of the story angle you're pitching. For example:

    • Cameron Herold has clients on three continents.
    • He's done speaking events in seventeen countries, on five continents.
    • He coaches entrepreneurs monthly.
    • He was the COO for 1-800-GOT-JUNK?, growing the company from $2 million to $106 million in six years.

Once you have approximately three angles and catchy titles set up with your supporting bullet points for each angle, and with main bullet points that you'll use on every pitch, then you're ready to call the media.

WHAT TO SAY TO THE MEDIA

When contacting the media, I've found that this simple script works best:

Start with: "Hi, my name is Cameron. Do you have a couple of minutes? I think I have a great story for you."

The writer will say one of the following:

(a) "Sure. What have you got?" To which you say: "Well, I have this cool story about this [fill in the blank]. Here are a couple of quick bullet points." Then, being the salesperson you are, you ask, "What do you think?" Continue to ask questions, and *listen*.

(b) "Sorry, I'm on a deadline." To which you say: "Okay. I'll call you tomorrow, or would the day after be better?" You also have the opportunity to ask what they're working on and listen to what they say. Suggest helpful options for achieving the writer's goals, and you'll be achieving your own at the same time. You can also suggest ways you could share expert comments for the current story.

(c) "No." To which you respond when the person hang ups on you: "Okay, so I'll just go grab a cup of coffee, sit down, and call the next person on my list." You're one call closer to a yes. In fact, skip the coffee and just keep cranking through the calls.

As the saying goes in sales (which I shared with you earlier in the context of making good communication a priority in your workplace), you have two ears and one mouth—use them in that ratio! The conversation should go something like this: you ask questions, you listen, you listen, you ask questions, you listen, and you listen some more.

Remember this, too: don't show up and throw up. Don't start giving the writer who answers the phone your entire story. Instead, quickly give the person your first little angle. Say, "What do you think?" The writer will give you an opinion right away, and then you'll narrow or amend your angle a little bit more or hit the writer with your second angle, or your third angle—which ever fits better. Stay alert and focused on the task at hand.

There really isn't much difference in terms of my approach for radio or blogs. In fact, in speaking with many bloggers, it's clear they're getting frustrated with people spamming them by email with story ideas; they'd love a phone call too. You can build great initial rapport with bloggers and journalists via Twitter, too. It's an easy way to get to know them so they'll write about you later. Making comments on blog posts that others write is another great way to get your name out there and raise your credibility.

If I have to leave a voice mail, I usually leave a message like this: "Hi Susan, this is Cameron Herold. Sorry I missed you, but I think I have a great story angle for you. I'll give you a call about it tomorrow. If you have a chance before then, you can call my cell: 604-351-9665."

Follow-up emails are fine for thanking the writers for their time. Follow-up emails are perfect after a writer covers you, but a handwritten thank-you note to him or her, *mailed* (as in placed in an envelope with a stamp), is 100 percent required. No one sends thank-you cards to just say thanks anymore, and you should—you'll stand out. (You know how important this is to me because I've mentioned it twice now in two separate contexts in this book!)

BUILDING YOUR PR TEAM

If you're reading this book, you're probably interested in performing these PR functions yourself or in hiring team members to perform them. This section will help you find the right people to execute the PR sales role in your organization and secure free exposure for your company.

In essence, what you're really hiring is a person who likes to do telephone sales. You're looking for someone who loves to pitch people. This individual must also be technically savvy enough to compile resources online and to track the media response to the system I've just described.

My first rule of thumb is this: *don't hire anyone with a PR background.* Typically, people with traditional backgrounds in PR are writers (or they wanted to be), and they will want to write newswires and press releases all day. There's nothing wrong with that, but what you want—and need— is someone who can deliver a persuasive sales pitch and follow up with everyone he or she contacts. It seems simple, but it's not. That's why I've included this list of skills and characteristics you'll want your PR team leader and/or members to have:

> **They've got to love to sell.** Candidates will need the ability to "get past the gatekeeper" in order to pitch. They should be able to raise and handle objections, track their own sales leads, and *love* to sell.
>
> **They have to be able to handle rejection.** Can they handle rejection and realize that "four noes are halfway to a yes"?

They must be energetic team players. I like to hire junior-level salespeople, who are usually in their mid-twenties and enthusiastic. Remember, you're not looking for people who can sell to VPs or CEOs.

They need to be able to listen. This involves the ability to understand what the writer wants to write about and come up with another angle on the fly. It's crucial that your PR person be able to make your stories fit.

They must be "glass half full" people. Find people who are optimistic, so their excitement and energy transfer to everyone they talk to, especially writers over the phone.

They need a great "phone voice." A great phone voice is important, not least because writers need to understand your PR salesperson. If these new hires will be pitching your business to writers in different regions, look for a team of people with accents that match your market, or at least have voices that are clear enough to appeal to people throughout North America.

They need to know how to write. Your PR people won't be writing press releases, but they will be doing tons of follow-up via email. Some of the best stories I've ever landed were from quickly scribbling a handwritten note to the journalist as well. It cuts through the clutter. Your PR team will have to be able to create excitement and get their point across succinctly.

They have to be tech-savvy. Since most of their resources will be online, PR salespeople will need to be skilled in the use of a computer and the Internet—which they'll be using for research constantly.

They need to be smart. The fact that this item is last doesn't make it any less important than the others. The people you hire to do PR work need to be information aggregators, intelligent enough to draw connections within the vast expanse of information they collect. Their research must be accurate, appropriate, and timely. They should love reading blogs and know how to use RSS and gather info from Twitter and other current social media. The information they gather this way is crucial to keeping them current on trends and supplying them with ideas they can include in pitches to writers.

The Sales Funnel

The number of calls you need to make before you land stories varies based on who you are, what your angle is, what's happening in the news, and how accurately you're targeting the writers. For example, your numbers will be horrible if you're calling writers who cover the oil and gas industry but you're pitching them about a small business angle. Even though they're business writers, none of them will ever cover you.

Assuming you are targeting writers who write your types of stories, in media outlets that have readers who would be interested in them, what follows is a rough estimate of the numbers you might expect from a PR person once that individual has been trained on your product, your company, and your industry. It takes a couple of months for even the best salesperson to know enough about the products and company he or she works for before he or she can close better than someone who's been with you for a year, so keep in mind that it doesn't happen overnight.

Monthly: You should expect five stories per PR person at a minimum.

Daily: Each PR sales team member makes six outbound pitches to journalists. Each pitch, most of which should be phone calls, includes these components:

- Taking notes from research on the target
- Recording what was said on the call
- Setting up follow-up times to call the writer back if necessary
- Verifying the writer's contact info
- Sending out follow-up information
- Following up with prospects from calls made in weeks prior

Tally: 6 calls a day × 5 days a week × 4 weeks a month = 120 outbound calls a month, which should generate five stories a month.

These numbers are pretty accurate and cover national, regional, and local media. They also cover spreading the calls out over TV, radio, print, online, newsletters, and bloggers. The numbers are pretty conservative too. If the angles are well thought out, and if the PR person sells well, he or she will land even more.

The only things your PR salespeople really need to track are these:

How many total stories are you landing monthly? Don't waste time tracking media impressions to come up with some fancy ROI. You'll know after six months that it works, and for the salaries and bonuses you're spending, you'll get great ROI. Spending time *overtracking* things just wastes time that you could spend pitching the media.

How many writers have you called back after the initial pitch? Keep a simple database in Microsoft Outlook, Sage ACT!, or a similar contact management system to track what you talked about and when you need to call the person back. Keep it simple.

Which writers will you contact again if they fail to express interest in your pitch the first time? If a writer shuts you down, you should always call on him or her again in the future with other ideas. I also call back such writers at a later date with perhaps a new twist on an old angle or when the business tide has changed to make that angle interesting again.

I've had the same writer cover me for different stories in different publications. Many writers freelance for a variety of publications, and they can cover your story in a few of them. Always continue to follow up until you're told to never call again!

If you really want to see results, start pitching the writers from the Associated Press, Bloomberg, and Dow Jones News Service. Even some of the regional papers work in syndicates, in which case your story could run in multiple papers. Pitching one person from the Associated Press could get you into more than one hundred papers that same week (versus trying to pitch a hundred writers). Leveraging can yield huge results.

Commission and Pay Structure

From my experience in building in-house PR teams, you need to look for junior-level salespeople who are just starting out. This group is looking to gain experience, work for a cool company, have flexible schedules, and so forth. Here's how I like to structure their pay. (Note: I'd even be fine with making the salary lower and the bonus amount higher once you know the rough numbers to expect.)

Salary: $40,000–$45,000 USD/year—this is as much as is needed (use equivalent amount for other countries).

Bonus: $500 USD/month ($6,000 USD annualized)—tied to the employee hitting five to eight stories a month. Don't set the bar too low (or too high).

Special bonuses: I've had awesome success with putting in a special bonus program to focus the efforts on landing top media outlets. List in advance which key outlets you want free PR in:

- Top five TV stations
- Top five radio stations
- Top five magazines
- Top five newspapers
- Top five websites or blogs

For each outlet, identify how much you're willing to pay extra for a full feature (i.e., a story about your business, with photo—not merely a brief mention in an article). This type of bonus, ranging from $250 to $1,000 per story, can generate a ton of focus.

A word of caution: don't let bonuses for major outlets take your employees' eyes off the prize. You still want each member of the PR team to land five to eight stories a month. The last thing you need is for a PR person to spend all his or her time trying to "bag the elephant."

A side story about success: one year I set up a bonus structure like this for a five-person PR team. They landed nineteen of the twenty outlets we'd identified on the list, and they split the bonuses they earned as a team. Plus, they hit 90 percent of the month's goals. Nice year.

—

As a final word on this subject, I'd like to leave you with this saying: "A shovel doesn't dig a hole." This really applies here. PR doesn't happen spontaneously: you have to use a plan like the one laid out here for it to work, and when you do, you'll get free PR. Remember to check out my website (www.BackPocketCOO.com) for an easy way to help you determine your business's first angle.

CHAPTER 9

FOCUSED PRODUCTIVITY

"The single-minded ones, the monomaniacs, are the only true achievers. The rest, the ones like me, may have more fun; but they fritter themselves away . . . Whenever anything is being accomplished, it is being done, I have learned, by a monomaniac with a mission."
—Peter Drucker, *Adventures of a Bystander*

Earlier, when I talked about reverse engineering, I discussed how to set broad goals and identify the projects you need to undertake to reach those goals. In this chapter, I will drill down deeper to help you develop the specific metrics you will need to monitor your progress toward your goal of doubling the size of your company—and, in the process, getting more of the right stuff done, by fewer people, faster.

Most companies measure either too many metrics or none at all. Even those companies that only measure a few key things rarely look at their numbers enough in any meaningful way to give themselves any insight into what they mean. We've all heard the saying "We can't manage what we don't measure." The key is figuring out the "Five Ws of Metrics":

- Who should measure metrics?
- What should you do with the data?
- When should you look at these numbers?
- Where should you store and track your data?
- Why should you measure at all?

Here are the absolute best basics to get you started. (Remember: don't turn this into a paper-pushing exercise or "analysis paralysis" either. *Keep it simple.*)

WHO SHOULD MEASURE METRICS?

You have to assign individuals in each business area of your company to be in charge of measuring and distributing the metrics for that area.

An easy way to accomplish this is to sit all the people from a business area in a room. The business areas for a company of $3 million in revenue should include sales, marketing, finance, IT, customer service, production, etc. Show the department members the company's key goals for the year, one of which will be to increase revenue by 25 percent. Then ask everyone to write down the metrics, or "Key Performance Indicators" (KPIs), they think their business area should measure. Once you have this all-inclusive list, you'll easily narrow it down to the ten to fifteen top KPIs—and even the five most critical, meaningful metrics for that area—by talking about each of them for half an hour as a group. In my experience, a little debate within the group allows you to figure out which numbers to really track as a company.

If you're trying to measure something intangible like employee or customer satisfaction, use the Net Promoter Score (which I introduced in the section called "Establish SMART Goals" in chapter 2). This is a simple process. Just asking the question "How enthusiastically would you recommend our company to your friends?" is enough to measure each area more completely than a dozen other metrics, especially when you are using the Net Promoter Score formula to calculate the results.

You will often hear the terms "leading indicator" and "lagging indicator" used in the discussion of metrics. Leading indicators give you a glimpse into what is coming your way by evaluating the past. Lagging indicators measure what's already taken place, but they don't forecast the future. You want to be able to track and measure numbers that give you both lagging and leading data and then use this data to support your decisions.

Once each business area's metrics are nailed down, you should be able to assign each of the metrics, perhaps two to three key numbers, to each person in that business area. When assigning each number to a person, make sure the person clearly understands that his or her "job is on the line"—the employee *must* ensure that the company hits that number. What are the key data points you can measure to help keep people focused, grade their performance, and keep them aligned with the important areas and numbers for the business unit in which they work?

Assigning one person as a single point accountable, or "SPA," for each metric is critical; it ensures that someone is accountable for each number you measure. This person will be responsible for the frequency of measuring important metrics, whether it's daily, weekly, monthly, or quarterly.

The key to making these metrics work is having a good SPA who will really dig into the different areas and grow the business rather than simply "playing businessperson" and just watching the reports. With regular attention to metrics, you'll be able to see important patterns, some of which may serve as warning signs or opportunities for growth. Often, as the company grows, I make the CFO responsible for *all* metrics reporting.

Remember: it's not about measuring everything. It's about measuring and monitoring the *right* things.

WHAT SHOULD YOU DO WITH THE DATA?

The next step is to assign a band of acceptability to the metric. What is the minimum result acceptable for each metric? What would indicate wild success?

So long as the data is within this range, the metric doesn't need to be looked at in-depth.

This simple practice of assigning a range for the data ensures that you don't have to spend countless hours looking at numbers that are moving along just fine. This way your team can spend time digging into the numbers that are too low or too high. The team can also leverage the numbers that are ahead of trend. For instance, years ago at 1-800-GOT-JUNK?, we were very far ahead of the profit forecasts we had set. We had a range identified, and if our profits were starting to look too large, a green flag would rise up, indicating that we were above the number we'd predicted. (The person entering the data assigned a color to each item: Green = Above Expectations; Yellow = Okay; Red = Missing/Below Expectations.) We were able to use some of the additional profits to continue to drive our revenues and growth even faster. Had we not been watching these leading indicators as closely, we might have missed the opportunity to leverage this profit.

Having a range allows you to take action according to the metric. If you don't have specific actions tied to specific metrics, you are just "playing business."

Measurement need not be too sophisticated: one simple thing I do to help decide what metrics to measure is to build a simple spreadsheet that shows the metric in question, who is responsible for it, when it will be reviewed, its status, and so forth. Each person who is accountable for a particular metric enters his or her data into the group's spreadsheet or dashboard.

WHEN SHOULD YOU LOOK AT THESE NUMBERS?

Once you know what key numbers (remember, I'm using the terms *metric*, *KPI*, *key number*, and *key data point* interchangeably throughout this chapter) to measure, you then need to decide how often the data will be reviewed.

If you are trying to double your revenues and profits (which you are), then being plus or minus a few points on a metric could really throw your ship off course. This means that you will have to review your metrics often and watch out for slight variations from your projections.

In every company I've helped to build since starting with College Pro Painters, I've looked at the KPIs every week. You want to be regularly looking at the numbers from your business because they will help you make the right decisions about what to really focus your time, employees, and money on.

Back in the College Pro Painters days, we called it the "weekly RAG," which stood for results at a glance. The RAG was critical to the goal setting and planning we did weekly to drive the business. If your current plan does not include a weekly look at a dashboard of your key data points, how's that working for you? I'll bet it's not. How many weeks do you let slip by without looking at all the key numbers for your business?

For each project in your organization's plan, there are key data points that should be monitored to ensure that all projects come in on time, on budget, and with the proper objectives achieved. One great way to ensure this is by collecting data along the way using a "5/15 reporting system."

How a 5/15 Reporting System Works

Every two weeks, have each of the individuals who report directly to you take fifteen minutes to write up a one- to two-page bulleted document that covers the status of each project for which he or she is responsible. They should spend no more than fifteen minutes on it, and it should take you no more than five minutes to read—hence the name. Each project should be marked with a green, yellow, or red dot showing whether it is on track, whether something is going wrong, or whether the project hasn't started yet. The 5/15 reporting system makes certain that you have visibility on all projects, which is, of course, preferable to finding out that something has gone off track when it's too late.

The bullet points I recommend that your employees include in their 5/15 reports are the following:

- Employees' goals for the upcoming week
- What they accomplished in the prior two weeks
- What's working in their respective business area
- What could be improved in their business area
- How they're feeling with the people in their group as a whole

Once a year, examine the frequency with which you are measuring and reviewing all the data and adjust how often you'll review each KPI going forward. Did you have enough data at your fingertips this past year? Would more or less frequency for each have helped you? Make sure you answer these questions.

WHERE SHOULD YOU STORE AND TRACK YOUR DATA?

Ideally, your company's metrics should be hosted live on a company intranet or in a web application that allows all your employees to view them, whether off-line or on. I've found that it usually works best to have a finance person pull the data together and make it look great and accessible on spreadsheets, while holding people in each business area responsible for ensuring the data for their respective area is updated regularly—and on time.

Each of the individuals responsible for one of the company's metrics should have his or her own dashboard that rolls up to an overall dashboard for the entire company. For example, marketing may have a mini-dashboard of perhaps ten to fifteen metrics they, as a department, measure and report on weekly and monthly to everyone in marketing. Each individual in an area should have his or her own dashboard too. I've often found the most effective ones are small whiteboards about the size of a computer monitor at each person's desk, where they track their own two to three metrics while keeping them visible for all to see.

Prior to building or purchasing dashboards or using dashboard software or web applications, start using good old Microsoft Excel or even the spreadsheet application in Google Docs. It will take you about six to twelve months of using and reviewing the data to really know how you want it to be represented.

At the end of the day, whatever dashboard you build, buy, or use should be easy to view. Only the outliers—the numbers that are below or above your specified threshold—should jump out at you. There is no sense in wasting time reviewing numbers that are right where you want them to be. Play with each metric over the course of a year and, if possible, ask other companies what they use. Check out dashboards on Google. Eventually, you'll find the right look and feel for your company.

WHY SHOULD YOU MEASURE AT ALL?

Facts and feelings are both clarified when real data is examined and analyzed on a regular basis. The simple sentence "You can't manage what you don't measure" couldn't be truer.

Measurement is key to making decisions. At 1-800-GOT-JUNK?, I felt that we were headed for growth problems because we were selling out our available territories in the United States. I knew that we'd be running out of areas to sell, and that our revenues and profits would be hurt if we didn't either start making the areas smaller or start selling internationally.

We just simply didn't have enough territories left to keep up our franchise sales growth rates.

However, the problem was that I couldn't get the rest of the team to listen to me. I didn't have the data at my fingertips. I just knew in my gut that what I was saying was true. Unfortunately, I left the company right around that time. Shortly thereafter, they found out that what I had been saying was, in fact, true, but they noticed it too late and had to cut people to offset the drop in revenues.

My own individual experience with lack of data shows how powerful data can be in proving your point—it can make you or break you. If we'd had the data at 1-800-GOT-JUNK? and if we'd reviewed it closely to look for this leading indicator, we might have had more foresight into how to plan for the drop. We wouldn't have had to *react*. In fact, the lack of data was so bad that our CFO at the time told me, "You just don't want to take accountability." She was new to the business and thought I was trying to avoid responsibility for this new area I'd just taken on. Far from it, actually: I knew the light at the end of the tunnel was a freight train coming at us, and the load was empty. We just didn't have much left to sell.

SHARE THE COMPANY'S INCOME STATEMENT

Years ago we read a book titled *The Great Game of Business*. It showed us that the income statement could be a great financial guide for the entire company. We would get all the employees together each month and give everyone a copy of the income statement, reviewing it line by line together. We'd look for areas to save money. We'd dig into all the expenses together as a team and look for ways to be more efficient. We'd work hard to have everyone treating the company as if he or she were an owner, and it was awesome to see the energy when everyone got to see the numbers together and work to improve the company as a whole.

—

In addition to using metrics effectively, another powerful way to improve your productivity is to leverage technology. Let's have a look.

CHAPTER 10

LEVERAGING TECHNOLOGY

"If the rate of change outside your business is greater than the rate of change inside your business, then you're out of business."
—Anonymous

Just last week I got an email from my dad, who is in his mid-sixties, in which he wrote, "The world is just moving too fast now because of technology." My reply? "Yeah, isn't it awesome? You just have to be riding the wave, though, or you'll get crushed by it." *So stop fighting it, and start riding the wave.*

The beautiful thing right now is that a great deal of the technology we can leverage is either free or very cheap compared to only five or ten years ago. We can use technology to cut costs we've been used to paying for years. Just last week I canceled my subscriptions to the *New York Times* and *Globe and Mail* newspapers because I now read them for free online from my iPhone. I've saved over $700 a year by doing that.

Leveraging technology is an opportunity for every company today. It offers us simple, low-hanging ideas to grow our businesses faster. The problem, however, is that most of us hate technology! I include myself in that group. The reason we hate technology is that we weren't raised with it. It's a little bit scary to us. It's a little bit intimidating to us. It's frustrating because it doesn't work the way we want it to (well, it *does* work, we just don't know how to use it). If you're in your late thirties to fifties, you're likely nodding your head in agreement with these statements.

So, I'm going to give you some lessons on how you can leverage technology in your business. And I highly recommend that you learn—and see to it that your employees learn—one little shortcut every week. It's incredible to me that so many people still use a mouse (even cordless ones) with their computer when so many shortcuts already exist simply by using the buttons on your keyboard (and they're proven to be faster).

To start off, keep it simple. Don't overthink things. If it feels complicated or expensive, it probably is. Look for simple "tech hacks" to get you started. These are simple shortcuts and ways to make your technology-enhanced life easier, and they're shared with us each day via blogs and social media sites such as Twitter. "R&D" (Rip Off & Duplicate) should be your mantra with regard to finding tech solutions to help your business. There is minimal ROI in you trying to figure out for yourself how to leverage technology when the experts already have the solutions for you. Just learn where to go to ask your questions!

SIMPLE TECHNOLOGY EVERYONE CAN LEVERAGE

Technology has this weird way of driving us all crazy when it should be helping us. It's gotten to the point with me where if it isn't simple, the IT guys pretty much have to bash me over the head before I let them try their new ideas. The ideas in this section are simple technology solutions that any company can use, and they are guaranteed to not drive you crazy.

Laptops

Get everybody in your business using a laptop. Get rid of your desktops. Laptops cost about the same. I've been using a laptop since 1994, and I now use a MacBook Air laptop that has a six-hour battery life. I can use it on all my flights. It's amazing. It has a backlit keyboard so I can use it in the dark and still see the keys. When everyone on a flight is watching a movie in darkness, I can work if I want to.

I can also sit and work from anywhere. I carry it from meeting to meeting. I take all my notes on it so I don't waste time rewriting notes back at my desk. It drives me nuts watching employees sit in meetings handwriting all their notes and knowing many will go back to their desks to "write everything up."

I gave laptops to all of my employees about nine years ago. The productivity gains we saw when they took the laptops home with them and worked for just a couple of extra hours a week was totally worth the investment.

Software

If you're thinking about building any new software in-house, really obsess about why you would be building it yourself. Depending on your industry, so much software already exists either for free or at such a low cost that building any custom software in-house just isn't worth it anymore.

Any software that you're plugging into your business should be the simplest option available. Most of the software out there has been overbuilt. Think about Microsoft Word. The only stuff that many of us really need in Microsoft Word might be templates, text formatting tools, editing features, and . . . what else? Not much. Get software that's simple to use. Obsess about *simplicity*, not extra *functionality*.

It's just like buying a VCR or a DVD player with functionality you never use. The more functionality you buy, the more confusing it gets to use. Strip down the complexity, and it all works—it's less confusing, and there will be fewer problems.

Three Monitors on Every Desk!

Bill Gates had a great idea with getting a computer on every desktop, but he fell short with that goal. Every company should have two to three *monitors* on every desktop!

Think about how many seconds each hour you wait for software or windows to open and close. Think about how many times a day you even open up a browser to look something up on Google. Add all of that open-and-close time together, and you'll see that you waste minutes each day. Those wasted minutes are completely obliterated by having multiple screens open at the same time. And additional monitors don't cost very much anymore—only around $150. The time saved and additional productivity gains well offset that small investment.

Use your additional monitors by having a web browser like Firefox open on one of them at all times, and keep Google as your homepage (you likely use it more than anything else). I keep Twitter as my homepage, and I have a little Google Search bar in Firefox so I get the best of both worlds. On your second monitor, keep your email open, but keep it open in draft mode. I also set up my email client to only find new mail manually. I don't want it reloading new messages as they arrive. I find that when I don't see new messages arriving it's a lot easier to check email only a couple times a day. The third monitor, my laptop, shows whatever application I'm working on at any given moment. Also, I've set up a tool called Spaces on my Mac so I can have nine application windows open and very quickly shift among them.

PDAs

You might have read the title of this section and thought, "PDAs? That's so 1999." It's true, it seems like ages ago when I first heard the term "PDA," or "personal digital assistant," but these portable devices have been around only since the mid-nineties. I purchased my first Palm 5000 in 1997 after seeing a friend of mine with one. His brother was the founder of PayPal, and he had one, too. I figured if smart guys like them were using PDAs, they had to be helpful. So I got one, and I was instantly connected, addicted, and more productive. Since then I've used Palm V, Treo, BlackBerry, and BlackBerry Pearl. For more than a year now, I've been using an iPhone.

Electronic tools such as these are powerful in business. This is the stuff that's allowing businesses to grow so quickly today. The main reason why some leaders aren't using them is simply because they haven't taken the time to learn about them. Don't let yourself off the hook if that's your excuse. Anyone in a management role in any company should be using an iPhone or BlackBerry. If you don't have one yet, get one! Synchronize it with your entire business. You'll have all your information at your fingertips. Be sure you turn off all the notifications, however. You don't need to know when every little email comes in; you don't need alarms for every single appointment. Use the PDA to control your *business*; don't let it control *you*.

Wireless Headsets

I've had a wireless headset for my office phone for about eight years. *Love* it. My favorites have all been manufactured by Plantronics, and I've updated my model a few times now from a great resource, Headsets.com.

I've always thought best on my feet and hated being chained to a desk. A wireless headset for my desk phone is awesome because I can pace while talking. I can go get a coffee or water; I can talk and move around. I even have one for my home office now, and I can go three floors down from my office and walk out to the car while on a call.

Whenever I'm talking to my lawyer on the phone, I go and flush the toilet just to make him think I wasn't paying attention! Scott always says, "Did you just flush the toilet?" To which I usually reply, "Yeah, that was the last invoice you sent me!"

Social Media

Social media can either be a great tool for companies or a complete waste of time and energy. I've been using it for years, and I know what fits for my company and what doesn't. I've spent time thinking strategically about how I can leverage components of it—and what not to use it for too.

First order of business? Get on Facebook. It may seem daunting at the start, but you'll figure it out, trust me! If you don't figure it out, it'll figure itself out for you. Put your business profile on Facebook and people will start finding you and linking to you. All of a sudden you'll realize that people are learning more about what you do—and remembering more about what you do—because of this social networking tool. Don't bother wasting time with all the silly stuff meant for teenagers. Think of Facebook as a résumé: an interactive, colorful one. Make sure it shows the best side of you, but more importantly, the *real* you. Start focusing your time on adding all the friends and business associates you know. If you start with that, and also spend time reading the messages people put up, you'll get the hang out of it. If it makes sense to do so (it doesn't for most), get someone in marketing or sales to set up and manage a Facebook fan page for your company.

LinkedIn is just like an online résumé. Get on there too! I've been on LinkedIn for close to ten years now. People aren't going to board of trade or chamber of commerce events to meet each other anymore. It's a waste of time. No one wants to pay for parking, walk into the gathering, talk to a bunch of suits, and come back out only to realize he or she has a pocket full of business cards to type up. *Eeeeew!* The new economy doesn't work that way. You'll meet a lot more people using free online technology.

You won't build one-on-one relationships using Facebook and LinkedIn, but you will identify potentially useful connections faster and will set up time to interact outside of LinkedIn. Set up your entire profile so that others can find you easily. When you or your team are hiring people, check out their profiles on both Facebook and LinkedIn too. You'll learn a lot about them.

Twitter is all over the media now. You can't miss it. I've been using Twitter since early 2008, and I rank in the top 2,500 people in the world to follow. Follow me, (@cameronherold) on Twitter, and you'll learn a ton about how to use the site for marketing and customer service. And it costs nothing. What's more, there are great free applications now that tie into Twitter and allow you to monitor what people are saying about you or your competitors. You can also regularly touch prospects and customers using Twitter. Some current tools, one of which is called Yammer, even allow you to use Twitter in private spaces. Set up Yammer and you can tweet inside your own company privately and have the same interaction you would on Twitter—just within your own parameters.

Recently, I've started using Twitter as a note-taking tool while at conferences. It allows me to multitask: I share with the people following me while reminding myself of the important points in a presentation. I type each idea or thought from a conference into Twitter. And at the end of the day, I simply copy and paste all of my tweets into a Word document. It's a great way to make Twitter work for you.

Blogging

Blogging can be a great way to share ideas with your customers and followers. It's an even better way to get your website ranking higher on targeted keywords. How do you know if you should blog? Start off by asking yourself these questions: Am I a thought-leader? Do I have the ability to write posts regularly? If you answered yes to *both* of those questions, start blogging. If you're not interested in leading discussions or don't have any time to update your blog, don't bother. It will just become another item on your To Do list, and it won't get the attention it deserves to actually be worthwhile.

If you decide to go ahead with blogging, it's crucial that you post often and create posts that are short enough so people can subscribe to your blog's RSS feed and get through them quickly. While the objective isn't to provide one-sentence entries—people want to learn from your posts, after all—you don't need to be writing a thesis in your blog posts. Keep your entries to five hundred words at the most. Anything more is too long, and people won't read it. Also, make sure you're using your targeted keywords in your blog posts so that when search engines "spider" the pages, they'll find the terms.

Sell Stuff Online

If you can sell your products or services off-line, you can probably sell some of them online too. I have been doing speaking events for groups of entrepreneurs for years, and many of them want to share the lessons they learn at my events with their employees. Now that I sell DVD recordings of my speaking events online, they can do this much more easily. With a simple setup through my website, companies in fifteen countries have purchased and begun using my DVDs. It has been a great success both for me and for the companies that find sharing these lessons with their employees useful. It also allows me to make money while I'm sleeping. Brilliant!

If you're going to be selling your services online, start with your website. Unless you dabble in web design, the simpler the interface, the better. That way, you don't have to update it often to maintain a fresh look. Instead of loading your site with useless content, figure out what you want your site to do for you, and provide content only for those areas. Got it? All I want people to do when they get to my website is to book me for speaking, to hire me for coaching, or to buy my DVDs. *That's it.* Make it easy for people to figure out how to do the things you want them to do when they get to your site, and leave it at that. You don't need anything fancy, just the facts.

Better Chairs

I decided to include this section in the chapter on technology because it is about the most technologically advanced chair there is.

One day I walked into my friend Kimbal's company in Boulder, Colorado. He was an employee of mine fifteen years ago, and he's been quite successful at building and selling companies since then. I couldn't help but notice the plethora of Herman Miller Aeron chairs—which used to go for about $800 USD.

When I got to Kimbal's office, I remarked, "Wow, you're really burning through cash on this new business of yours!"

He looked at me, perplexed. "Why do you say that?"

"I saw your Herman Millar Aeron chairs everywhere!" I was convinced he was already spending the millions he'd made in business. I love Herman Miller chairs—I even have one—but I couldn't imagine buying one for every employee.

So then Kimbal asked, "You didn't see the desks did you?"

I hesitated. "No, I didn't see the desks."

"Go take a look," he said knowingly. I walked outside, took a look, and noticed he had all these white plastic fold-up tables pulled up to those fantastic and expensive Herman Miller chairs.

"What's with all of the fold-up tables?" I said upon reentering Kimbal's office.

He paused for a moment before answering. "Well, everyone wants to have an amazing chair. You want to attract amazing employees? Don't give them a $200 chair. You want to keep all of your employees happy? Don't give them a $200 chair. Everybody out there buys $1,000, $2,000, $3,000 workstations or desks, and then they buy crummy $250 chairs. So I buy a shitty $50 table from Costco, and I buy an awesome $800 chair, and my employees love me. They never quit. They tell everybody about it, and everybody walks in and sees we're successful, but they don't realize we spent $850 on my desk and chair while everybody else spent $3,000. Do the math!"

Ever since the day I learned that lesson from Kimbal, I've been telling every CEO I meet to buy those chairs for their employees too.

GETTING STUFF DONE REMOTELY

In our parents' era, you hired employees to do work for you. Or, at best, you hired a company nearby to which you could farm out work. Now you can get stuff done by professionals around the world.

How does it work? You post the projects or work you need done, and people around the world start bidding on the project, offering their price to get the work done for you. They even provide references and samples for past work they've done. I've used virtual assistants around the world to work on miscellaneous tasks for me. Over the last year alone, for instance, I've had research done by someone living in Karachi, Pakistan, for $2 an hour. I needed to get some contact info, addresses, and information related to venture capital firms and angel investors in Washington State and British Columbia. It would've taken me all week to do it. And I could have had an employee do it, but that cost was so much more than outsourcing the task.

During the same year, I wanted to get all of my DVDs from speaking events transcribed, so I used the transcription services of someone in Sweden for $8 an hour. I also had some media interviews that included content I thought could be useful, so I simply emailed my Swedish transcriber the files and she typed them all up in Word for me. Many transcription firms used to charge $125 an hour for this. The Swedish woman's twenty hours of work was a little more than $125 total.

CEOs I mentor are starting to outsource work they used to delegate to employees. It just doesn't make sense to assign work to people for three to ten times what it costs us to outsource using websites like this. As long as you're getting the right quality out of such services, it's worthwhile.

Here are companies I recommend that you investigate the next time you have a task you can outsource.

Guru.com, eLance.com, Amazon's Mechanical Turk—all these are great services for getting miscellaneous admin and technical tasks done by remote workers around the world. These services work the same way as eBay, where you list stuff you want to sell and people bid on what they will pay for it. You simply post the project that you need done, when you need it done, and people bid on what they are willing to do the work for. You'll get references and samples of prior work, and often you can get work done for one-tenth of what you'd pay a full-time employee in North America.

Outsourcing Things Done—Based in Manila, this company hires and manages executive assistants. In fact, they interviewed and trained my assistant, Melanel Perez, for me. (She had also earned a business degree from one of the top schools in the Philippines.) I assign tasks to her weekly, and she cranks through them as though she were working next to me in my company's offices. We communicate via Outsourcing Things Done's proprietary "Wiki & Task" software as well as Skype video and email. This sure beats paying someone who lives in North America $40,000 a year when I can get the same work done by Melanel for $1,200 a month (or $14,400 a year).

Crowdspring and 99designs—These are both great services for when you need to get random items (brochures, flyers, employee recognition plaques, web pages) designed. You post your project description and what you are willing to pay, and people from around the world submit designs to you, hoping to be chosen. You pay for only the designs you choose. Crowdsourcing sites such as these produce high-quality marketing work, done cheaply and quickly.

HOW TO FIGURE OUT TECHNOLOGY

Here's how you figure out technology: hire a bunch of twenty-five-year-olds! Seriously. What are any of us trying to figure it out for? The Millennials and their slightly older brothers and sisters already know it! They're vastly more adept at understanding technology, and we can learn a lot from them. Let me illustrate.

I was in an Apple store in Portland, Oregon, last year to purchase a laptop bag, and when I was ready to check out, I looked around saying, "Where's the cashier? There's no cashier!"

My thirty-three-year-old buddy Josh, who was standing beside me, said, "They're different here!"

"Umm, really?" I said. "There's no freaking cashier. That's definitely different!"

Josh then instructed me to put my hand up, which I did, because he seemed to know what was going on. As soon as I did, two people came rushing over with these little handheld terminals, and they each asked, "Would you like to cash out?" Obviously, yes. So one of them took my merchandise, scanned the tags, swiped my credit card, and said, "Would you like me to email you a receipt or would you like me to print one out right now?"

"Email would be good," I said.

"Thanks for shopping with us!" the friendly Apple person said. And that was it. No waiting in line, nothing.

This is a story I've shared many times at speaking events, because many of my audiences are doing stuff a little bit differently too. They're hiring a bunch of twentysomethings who understand technology, and they're leveraging that in their business. They're making everything go a little bit faster, a little bit more efficient, and they're getting people—both within and outside the company—to talk about technology. These tech-savvy staff members are the ones you should be looking to hire at all levels of your company too. I've had a lot of men and women in their mid-twenties make fantastic managers and leaders of teams for me.

Listen: *you're not going to figure out technology.* I'm not either!

If you can't find tech-savvy younger people in real life to hire, try finding them on Facebook. And don't overlook the employees who are already in your company. Go for lunch once or twice a month with someone in his or her twenties (if you can coax the techie into it). Ask him or her to teach you some little tech hacks to make your business run simpler and faster, and in exchange, you can mentor the junior staffer on how to build a company. It's a great trade-off for both of you.

Your twenty-five-year-old can help you keep up-to-date with the latest technology tools. Things are being developed so rapidly that you may need more than one assistant to help you out. Here are just a few technology tools that I have found to be very useful.

Ambiance—This is a simple app for the iPhone that plays background sounds at night when you're on the road, trying to fall asleep in a strange hotel room. I used it recently while staying at the Driskill Hotel in Austin, Texas, which is supposedly haunted. Falling asleep while listening to waves rolling up on shore made sleep easier than worrying about ghosts or listening to traffic ten stories below.

TimeScroller—This great free tool, which is both an app for iPhone and a widget for Macs, allows you to see multiple time zones at the same time. You just scroll over with the mouse or touchscreen and it shows you when meetings can be set up at times that make sense for people in different time zones, countries, cities, etc. I find this super-helpful when setting up conference calls with clients in Europe, Asia, and Australia.

Tungle.me—This free online app lets you seamlessly schedule meetings without double-bookings, time zone mishaps, and endless back-and-forth emails. It lets you easily schedule meetings at times that suit all the attendees, both inside and outside your organization, and you can invite others to schedule a meeting with you even if they aren't signed up on Tungle. They simply look at your free and busy slots. All they can see is whether you are free; they can't see any details about the appointments you've booked.

Dragon Dictation—The iPhone app is fantastic. It allows you to leave a voice note—even in a busy bar—and seconds later it appears transcribed for you to save, copy, email, etc. And it's free. I used to use other apps like Jott and Google Voice to do this, but Dragon is my new favorite.

Duo and TweetDeck—These are two great apps that let you update your status in multiple places, such as Twitter, Facebook, and LinkedIn, at the same time. Duo is for the iPhone. TweetDeck has both iPhone and free software downloads for your computer too.

CardSnap—This is a wonderful and simple app for iPhone that allows you to take a photo of a business card. The data on the business card is then automatically imported into your database using optical character recognition (or OCR in techie parlance). At $5, this is *way* better than any scanner I've used.

Bump—This app is an easy way for two people with iPhones to exchange contact info. If they both have Bump, two users can literally bump their phones together, and each user's contact info is placed in the other's address book automatically (not including the notes section of the contact).

Automator—Macs have a built-in software program called Automator that allows you to automate tasks (similar things can be done with a PC). For example, if you open the same six applications each time you start your computer, why not have it set up to open them automatically for you?

Skype—We've been waiting for years to play with the technology we saw on *The Jetsons*. Now you can use it for free. Why use a telephone to make sales calls or customer calls? Skype video calls are a fantastic way to keep building the relationships between you and your team, clients, or prospects. Something extra happens with the face-to-face communication.

Basecamp—This is fantastic project-management software. Simple to use. Easy to access. And far less cumbersome than any of the big project-management tools companies waste time using.

Help a Reporter Out (HARO)—This free service, which I mentioned in chapter 8, sends you emails daily from writers around North America who are looking for experts to contribute to stories they are writing. It's an easy way to grow your brand.

LinkedIn—As I mentioned earlier in this chapter, this is a great way to get introduced to people at other companies. It is also a great way to read up on people you are thinking of hiring.

RSS Readers—Don't waste time going to each individual blog you read. Set up an RSS feed from all the blogs you want to read and have them all set up in an RSS reader, such as NetNewsWire, that downloads all the blog posts to one place and has them synchronized both on your laptop and iPhone. That way you can read them when you have spare time to kill rather than reading them while you're at your desk trying to focus on a project.

Teamly—This is a great new tool, which you can access at Teamly.com, for managing your top five priorities, and those of your team as well. It sends you reminders and forces you into the habit of setting your top five goals daily and weekly. I'm now an actual shareholder of this company.

Google Docs—There is no need to keep purchasing software applications like Word and Excel for your employees. Google Docs gives you these applications for free. If you need to share a spreadsheet or document that incorporates features only available in Word or Excel, you can have one version of the real thing running on a shared computer in the company lunchroom. Why pay for software licenses year after year when you can get the same tools free of charge in the cloud?

There are numerous other tools that will also increase your personal productivity. I have included a list of these items on my website (www. BackPocketCOO.com), and I'm always looking for more.

—

You have to keep up with technology in order to double the size of your business. But you might ask yourself, "What good is all this technology if the economy is zooming downhill?"

I'll answer that question in the next chapter.

CHAPTER 11

HOW TO GROW WHEN IT'S SLOW

"Never miss out on an opportunity like a good recession."
—Jack Welch

STOP IT!
STOP IT!
STOP IT!

Stop complaining and stop making excuses. So what if the economy sucks? Yes, there is a recession. Yes, the housing market has plummeted. I know. *I get it.* I read more news from multiple outlets than I probably should. I don't care that the economy sucks and neither should you. Refuse to participate in recessions. I've been predicting an even worse double-dip recession for months now. Who cares?

I know that it's difficult when every economist, political pundit, and news reporter is talking about the recession. You have to remember that media hype is not an accurate reflection of reality. It's a vision of reality that is distorted to make it more dramatic and to attract viewers. Stop being distracted by the media. Stop focusing on the word "recession" and obsessing over the unknown. As an entrepreneur, you should realize that the unknown will always be a part of your life. Your job is to stay focused and double the size of your company.

I was speaking a while ago in San Francisco to a group of entrepreneurs from all over the United States. It was a four-hour workshop on how to grow your company and foster an awesome culture. Some of these entrepreneurs had sixteen employees in their company, some had 160 employees, and a few had a couple thousand. What they had in common, however, was their intention to grow roughly 20 percent in 2009. That date put them in the throes of a recession, but they didn't care. Yet, they kept talking about the downturn in the economy in spite of the fact that they all planned to grow their businesses. Finally, I told them that every time I mentioned the word "economy" during the four-hour session they were to scream "STOP IT!" loudly at me. We practiced a few times, and they were really loud for sure. I never mentioned the word for the rest of the presentation. Everyone should play this little game with themselves: every time you hear yourself saying either "economy" or "recession" silently scream "STOP IT!" to yourself. When you have the word recession on your mind, it prevents you from thinking positively and focusing on growth—especially doubling your company in three years or less!

The reality is that there has been a huge slowdown, and when it runs its course, we'll all learn that it was worse than anything we've gone through since the Great Depression. However, the smart and focused entrepreneurial companies will work around it and will still do quite well. We may have another recession somewhere down the line, and if we do, there's no reason to behave any differently from how we do this time.

When you read the advice of Jack Welch that opened this chapter—"Never miss out on an opportunity like a good recession"—did you ask yourself why such an accomplished businessperson as this former CEO would say something like that? Keep reading to learn some counterintuitive tips—and some boring but essential tips—about growing during an economic slowdown.

THE TOP TEN WAYS TO MAKE MONEY IN A RECESSION

I've divided the ten tips into two sections: first, six counterintuitive pieces of advice, and second, four boring but tried-and-true ideas. All of the ideas work, but a few of them will feel contradictory to what you may have heard is the "right" way to behave in business, and that's the point: while everyone else is shutting down production, you're going to be planting the seeds for growth.

Counterintuitive Tips

Each of the six items in this section is contrary to what you would expect, particularly when sales are slow, but I promise you they can yield significant results as you march toward the goal of increasing your growth by 25 percent every year for the next three years.

Tip 1: Increase your expenses.

Because personnel is generally the largest line item in any company's budget, a surefire way to increase your expenses is to increase the number of people who work for you and/or reward the ones already in your employ.

Hire another salesperson. When your competitors are slowing down and grumbling about the recession, they start worrying their employees. When competitors start laying people off, the great employees fear for their jobs too. If you're hiring salespeople when everyone is laying them off, the positive buzz that you're still hiring will start to spread. What's even better? Imagine hiring one of your competitor's best salespeople. It would impact both of your companies in precisely the way you want to in a competitive world. I know it seems odd that while in the middle of a recession you'd want to hire more people, but the people you will be hiring are the rainmakers. You're hiring people to increase sales, add money to your gross margin, and increase buzz about your company and brands.

Give everyone a raise. Make raises 100 percent commission based, but give everyone a stake in finding new business. Hell, even accounting and IT teams can find clients, so create an upside for them too. When everyone in your company has a stake in the outcome and can make more money by bringing in clients or employees, they will work to help you build your business. Also, teach your employees how to network. Give them marketing pieces with a promo code customizable to that employee. Help them make more money, and you will too.

Tip 2: Fire your customers.

Eighty percent of your results come from 20 percent of your clients; so, at minimum, fire 20 percent of your clients. They are sucking up 80 percent of your time. Feels odd to be thinking about getting rid of some of your revenues at any time, let alone during an economic downturn, but these clients likely generate very little revenue, and perhaps even cost you money. So get rid of them.

If you're wondering which clients to fire, ask your sales, finance, and customer service employees which clients they'd like to eliminate. Generally they'll all have the same list. It's not about perfection here, either; it's about eliminating the obvious ones.

In cutting these bottom-20-percent clients (particularly the ones who don't pay their bills), you'll also be eliminating some of the waste or overhead you have in supporting them. You'll free up time in all areas of your business, especially shipping, customer service, and accounting. You'll also save time in your sales meetings by not talking about these deadbeat clients. You'll free up more time for your profitable clients and get more business from your best ones.

Tip 3: Someone has money, so go get some of it.

Strong companies and rich clients *always* have money.

The statement above rings true even in recessions. In fact, that's where the old adage that "cash is king" in a recessionary market comes from. Many companies saw this coming and moved into cash a long time ago. They've been waiting for deals. They've been waiting for the market to turn. They're also waiting to buy from you. *Sell to them*. They've got money. Some of it could be yours.

So, how do you get some of that money? I'll answer that question by starting with a story. Years ago, one of my sales teams was working with a large client called Public Storage. We were doing about $180,000 of business with them annually. When we asked them how much total spending they did with us and with competitors of ours, they said they'd have to check. The following week they came back and reported that overall, company wide, they spent about $2 million. Wow! And we were getting a mere 9 percent of that!

Imagine how the conversation changed at that point to this: "How can we get more of your business? What do you need to see from us to spend 50 percent of that figure with us?" We knew they had the money because they told us they were spending it! Now we just needed to work closely with them to have them spend it with us instead of our competitors.

Figure out which of your clients or prospects are doing well. Do your research, really focus on those prospects, and you'll land them without any problem. Ask your clients how much of their current business you are currently getting. Spending time with your top clients to increase revenues is easier than finding new ones. They've got money, remember, and more of it could be yours.

Tip 4: Eliminate competitors.

Ray Kroc grew McDonald's from a few locations to the enormously powerful brand we all know (and secretly crave). He also had a particularly cutthroat saying about business: "When the competition is drowning, stick a hose in their mouths." Though brutal, Kroc understood that the best time to eliminate his competitors was when they were weakest—during an economic downturn when they had left themselves vulnerable.

I once saw a Nike T-shirt that said: "Somewhere, right now, someone is practicing. When they meet you head to head in competition, they'll beat you."

This seizing on vulnerability is where business is most like sports—your competition is naturally your opponent. When you come to the game unprepared for the challenge, someone will be there waiting for you to choke, and when you do, they'll happily leave you on the sidelines while they advance toward their goal. Hiring competitors' salespeople, proactively targeting your competitors' clients, and even repricing your products or services to attract those clients will help you and hurt your competitor.

Tip 5: Start stealing—legally.

Customers will switch from your competitors right now for even the *smallest* discounts or bonus offers, so steal them away. You can't go so far as predatory pricing, but in a slowdown, virtually everyone is looking to save a buck. So target your competitors' customers and start offering them what it takes to get them to move to your business. Over time, you'll be able to raise your prices.

Tip 6: Find money under your company's pillow.

You've already got lots of products or services, so why not re-brand them or remarket them? For example, I sell leadership DVDs that are used by CEOs and their employees around the world. Once I started selling them as a package of four, DVD sales really took off. "The Back-Pocket Packet" accounts for 90 percent of the orders fulfilled from my website today.

Another area to find cash under your company's pillow is by considering selling off a small equity position in your company. You'll be able to realize some cash for what you've built already, and you could have a major opportunity if you sell a small position to either a current or large supplier or customer. If they own 5 percent of your business, you'll get 100 percent of theirs.

Tried-and-True Tips

If you tend to be risk-averse, you'll probably be more comfortable reading these four ways to make money in a recession than you were considering the six counterintuitive tips.

Tip 7: Stay positive.

There *will* be a long slowdown or recession—so what? We're going through a much-needed correction in the market, and the strong will come out of it even stronger. In every recession, companies still do well. Choose to be one of them. Remember: like attracts like. Stay positive and you attract positive things. If you're down and gloomy you won't attract anything worthwhile.

Tip 8: Stay focused.

Don't keep adding stuff to your To Do list. If anything, start crossing stuff that doesn't need to be done off your list. For example, if it won't have an impact on sales going up, profits going up, or costs going down—*stop doing it*.

Each morning (or the night before), write down the top five things you need to get done that day. Then start working on number one until it's done. Then move on to number two. If you are diligent and stay focused using this age-old method, you and your team will grow during any downturn we have.

I also advise that you follow the 80/20 rule. We all know and accept that 80 percent of the results come from 20 percent of the work. I like to use that as a way to focus myself, too. For example, if you had only two hours a day to get work done, what would you want to get done right away? Do you know what that activity might be? Okay, do that, and that alone. Imagine if, for eight hours a day, you worked solely on those crucial tasks versus being distracted by the numerous other items that seem to spring from out of nowhere each day.

Tip 9: Reinforce your relationships.

The great thing about an economic slowdown is that it gives you more time. You can use this time to reinforce relationships inside and outside your company. Inside the company, take the time to get to know people better. Indulge them in activities you know they enjoy. Bring employees along with you to board meetings, divisional meetings, or strategic planning sessions. Take people for coffee who you don't normally ask. Set up random lunches a few times a month and invite three to five employees you rarely spend time with. It all makes a huge difference when you are trying to grow.

Get more from each of your current clients by building relationships with them. Get to know their companies, their needs, and a bit about their personal lives. Protect these clients and you will generate tons of referrals and introductions.

As Greig Clark used to say, "People by day, paper by night." The paperwork and emails can wait; your customers won't. Get away from your desk and out of email and build real relationships in person.

While everyone else is complaining and worrying about the economy, get out there to market and advertise your business. Get noticed. Find a few fun and free ways to call attention to yourself and your company. It drives me nuts when people think they are "too professional" to do guerilla marketing. Some of the biggest and fastest-growing brands on the planet are doing that very thing. Grasshopper, a company just outside of Boston, Massachusetts, made a huge splash in the spring of 2009 when it sent real chocolate-covered grasshoppers to five thousand tech geeks and entrepreneurs. Included in the package of grasshoppers was a URL for an inspirational video that eventually went viral from all of the attention it received. The company was featured in tons of media outlets and generated a lot of buzz and sales. If you're going to do guerilla marketing, don't play it safe!

Tip 10: Watch your cash flow.

Look for all the areas in which you can cut expenses—except advertising and marketing. Obviously, if you cut those, you will see a slowdown of your own making. Really look for waste in your company and start cutting it fast anywhere you can. Cut the people you've been wanting to fire but didn't have the guts to. Cut any "dead weight employees."

Increase credit lines at your bank and with credit card companies—now, and every six months for as long as you're in business. Stop buying stuff. Really. Put a freeze on virtually all the spending you can. You'll be amazed at how much money you free up just by saying no to virtually all potential expenses. Tighten the belt fast.

Collect from customers faster than you used to, but be gentle and selective in doing it. Collect COD as much as possible. Get customers to prepay. Increasing your cash flow at times is as good or better than cutting expenses.

Pay your bills slower than you used to. Delay paying receivables as long as you can. Even just waiting until the last few days allowed will make a big difference.

—

The most important thing to remember in bad times is to keep up your spirits. I live by this slightly tweaked version of an old adage: *"Early to bed, early to rise, work like hell and advertise."* It always helps me get through downturns.

The good news is that bad economic times will only make strong companies stronger. If you never lose sight of your Painted Picture and focus on your company's growth rather than the overall economy, your business will thrive. In the next part of the book—which is about focusing on leadership, the third actionable step in the doubling process—I will show you how you yourself can thrive during this fast-paced growth.

PART 3

FOCUS ON LEADERSHIP

CHAPTER 12

THE ROLLER-COASTER RIDE OF ENTREPRENEURSHIP

"First, and most importantly, realize that a start-up puts you on an emotional roller coaster unlike anything you have ever experienced."
—Marc Andreessen, cofounder of Netscape

This chapter is about the emotional realities of being an entrepreneur and what you're going to be feeling during the journey toward doubling your company. I'm not talking about what's in your head; I'm talking about what's in your gut, and how to use and learn from those feelings inside that human computer of yours to help you become really successful.

It's important that you understand this roller coaster, and the people you work with must understand it as well. As an entrepreneur, your attitude and actions dramatically affect the company culture. If those around you understand the roller coaster you are riding, they will be better prepared to enjoy the ride and help you focus on the Painted Picture.

You will flip rapidly from a day in which you are euphorically convinced you are going to own the world, to a day in which doom seems only weeks away and you feel completely ruined, and back again. Over and over and over.

And I'm talking about what happens to stable entrepreneurs.

There is so much uncertainty and so much risk around practically everything you are doing. Will the product ship on time? Will it be fast enough? Will it have too many bugs? Will it be easy to use? Will anyone use it? Will your competitor beat you to market? Will you get any press coverage? Will anyone invest in the company? Will that key new engineer join? Will your graphic interface designer quit and go to Google? And on and on and on . . .

Some days, things will go really well, and on other days, things will go really poorly. And the level of stress that you're under will generally magnify those transient data points into incredible highs and unbelievable lows at whiplash speed and huge magnitude.

Sound like fun?

Most entrepreneurs say yes to at least five of the following questions. Do you?

- Are you filled with energy?
- Does your mind get flooded with ideas?
- Are you driven, restless, and unable to keep still?
- Do you often work on little sleep?
- Can you be euphoric?
- Are you easily irritated by minor obstacles?
- Can you burn out periodically?
- Do you act out sexually?
- Do you feel persecuted by those who do not accept your vision?

Many extremely successful entrepreneurs are even clinically diagnosed as manic-depressive, or having bipolar disorder (nicknamed the "CEO disease"). Francis Ford Coppola has it. So does Ted Turner. Jim Clark, co-founder of Netscape, was described in *BusinessWeek* by Netscape's former president and CEO, Jim Barksdale, as someone "who has his mania only partly under control. He's a perpetual motion machine with a short attention span, forever hurtling at unsafe speeds. When his forward motion is impeded, Clark becomes irritable and bored. In his search for the stimulation of the 'new, new thing,' he quickly loses interest in the companies and ideas he starts and tosses them into the laps of his bewildered employees."

Apple CEO Steve Jobs has been described as "hypomanic" and unable to think outside the box because he doesn't even see the box. He's also been described as quick to fly off the handle emotionally.

CEOs and entrepreneurs rarely go public with their stress or depression, as neither builds confidence in their ability to run the business. However, CEOs' notes on blog sites, or their status updates on Twitter, Facebook, or LinkedIn, will commonly include comments such as these:

- I haven't been able to accomplish anything so far this week.
- I can't shake this depression long enough to do what I know needs to get done.
- I can't sleep. Two hours last night. It's only when my body can't go on any longer that I sleep.
- I know what needs to be done. I just don't have what it takes today.
- I'm trying to take things one day at a time.
- I wish I'd done more to keep in touch with my friends instead of being such a workaholic.
- Last week I was a whirlwind. This week I'm doing nothing.
- My mind is sluggish. It's taking me a great deal of time to accomplish even the simplest of tasks.
- Something needs to change pretty soon or I won't be able to crawl out from under my rock.
- This is not a good day. I hope tomorrow is better.

Regardless of whether or not you believe you will ride a roller coaster while running a business, you will! Trust me. It doesn't matter whether it's Richard Branson, Bill Gates, or my sister starting her own business— no matter who you are, you're going to ride the monster roller coaster of entrepreneurship! The key to riding it out is that you've really got two choices: you can hold on and scream, or you can wave your hands in the air and have fun.

THE TRANSITION CURVE

I didn't come up with the idea of the Transition Curve. I've never been smart enough to come up with a model like this on my own! But over the twenty-some years since I saw it for the first time, I've added to it and adapted it to fit our subject matter, entrepreneurship. (Perhaps you, too, have seen one of the numerous variations of this model that circulate under the same name.) What I was actually smart enough to do with this model was to figure out what entrepreneurs should or shouldn't do when they are at each stage. It's one thing to identify the feelings at each stage, but it's another thing entirely to know what to do when you're on the ride itself.

Transition Curve

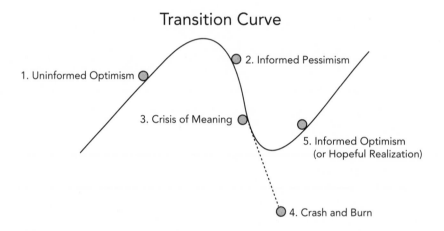

1. Uninformed Optimism
2. Informed Pessimism
3. Crisis of Meaning
4. Crash and Burn
5. Informed Optimism (or Hopeful Realization)

Stage 1: Uninformed Optimism

The first stage of the concept is called Uninformed Optimism. When you're at this stage on a real roller coaster, just when you're getting to the top of the curve, adrenaline is pumping through your veins and you're experiencing feelings of excitement and nervous energy, among others.

In the world of running your own business, you're excited and filled with energy and passion at this stage, and it's fun. No coffee is needed. You don't really know what's coming next, but you're excited about the future. Your excitement alone is enough to get you out of bed, to keep you from going to sleep, and to keep your entire team and your customers pumped up. Although the excitement is built on the unknown, you think you're invincible at this stage.

This optimism should not be discouraged, but entrepreneurs need to recognize that's what they're feeling, and they should harness and use it to be successful. If you're being coached or mentored by someone at this stage, don't let that individual oversell or overexcite you. You don't want them contributing to your already unrealistic expectations. Just harness the energy you already have.

Also, recognize that this enthusiasm and optimism won't last. In the near future, it will change, and you will become increasingly disappointed, discouraged, and pessimistic. That's normal.

Stage 2: Informed Pessimism

The second stage in the Transition Curve is Informed Pessimism. As you ride over the top of the curve, you've now got a little bit more information, and as a result, you have feelings of fear, nervousness, and frustration. You might even want to get off the ride. You're thinking, "I'm not really sure what's coming yet, but I'm getting a little nervous in my gut about it!"

You'll begin to become slightly more pessimistic about your whole business. You'll focus more on the shortcomings. Your glass starts looking half empty instead of half full.

Stage 3: Crisis of Meaning

Then you hit a stage called Crisis of Meaning. This is when you're really scared. You're in despair. It's like standing on the edge of a cliff ready to jump. Your thoughts might be something like this: "Today the roller coaster's going off the bottom of the track for the very first time. I'm going to die!" You'll feel helpless. You'll feel terrified and frozen.

Stage 4: Crash and Burn

If you don't pull through the bottom of the curve and round the corner, then you will Crash and Burn. This fourth stage in the Transition Curve is when you go bankrupt, are forced to sell, or are faced with some other horrible catastrophe.

Sometimes it takes a massive amount of effort, tears, and tenacity to pull through this stage. If you're working closely with a good coach, he or she should be able to help you identify in advance all of the support groups or activities that you can use to reduce stress and turn these situations around.

This is often a stage at which franchisees do much better than solo companies. In the franchising world, most franchisors are good at helping franchisees avoid big problems because they have seen them so many times already with other franchisees. Eighty-five percent of all solo businesses fail within the first year. And something like 85 percent of the surviving 15 percent fail in the next four years. The odds aren't good that you're going to get through this whole curve.

The people who do actually get through it are the ones who recognize they are starting to have those feelings and then quickly turn for support from whomever can help. You just have to ride it out, and believing that you can get through the other side is important.

It reminds me of the Chinese proverb "Fall seven times, stand up eight." We can't get off the roller coaster; we have to keep getting through the stages as productively as possible.

Stage 5: Informed Optimism (or Hopeful Realization)

At the final stage, Informed Optimism, you're calm and informed. You might even say you are cautiously optimistic.

WHAT TO DO AND WHAT *NOT* TO DO AT EACH STAGE

At each stage of the curve, you can leverage the feelings and energy—positive or negative—that you have at that moment. Opportunity and danger exist at every stage. Or you can fight against the feelings and energy, but that's like working against gravity, which depletes you and your reserves fruitlessly. Learn to become gravity's ally and go with the flow.

Stage 1: Uninformed Optimism

This is a great place and a dangerous place, depending on what you're working on at the time. For example, this stage is an excellent time for you to "be on stage," that is, talking to the media. If a newspaper reporter calls you when you have Uninformed Optimism, the interview will go amazingly well because you'll be gushing with excitement and positive energy that will come across in the finished piece. Your unbridled passion and enthusiasm will have the journalist wanting to invest in your company. I've even had writers interviewing me at this stage say things like, "Wow, this is awesome! Are you guys hiring?"

The reason everyone got so caught up in the mania of the nineties dot-com bubble was that we got carried away with the dreams and energy of all those entrepreneurs and start-ups. Passion can be contagious.

In chapter 10, I introduced you to a former employee, Kimbal Musk, and his brother Elon, founder and chairman of PayPal. In 1994 they were raising money for their first cofounded company, Zip2. (They also had the domain name www.x.com: think about how early they were to enter the Internet game!) When Kimbal told me about the company they were building, he was gushing with optimism. Several times during the call he said, "We don't even know what we're doing yet, but we'll figure it out as we go. We're sleeping in the office and showering down the street at the gym." A few years later they sold the company for $315 million in cash. Their optimism carried them.

In early 2009, I shared the stage with Morten Lund, the initial investor and cofounder of Skype. He had recently gone personally bankrupt and lost $40 million of his own cash, but he was positive nevertheless. "I was mad at myself for a few minutes, but then realized I own parts of eighty other companies already so I know I'll make it all back. I don't know how yet, but I know I will." Those are the kinds of Uninformed Optimistic comments entrepreneurs need to be making to rally their teams through the tough times and the craziness of growth.

When Jeff Bezos was launching Amazon in the mid-nineties, he used to jump up and down while presenting because he was so excited. He was also roughly $1 billion in debt, but you'd never have known it. This is a prime example of why this stage can also be dangerous. Spending money is a bad thing to be doing during Uninformed Optimism. It's why so many companies blew up in the dot-com era after spending millions on Super Bowl ads.

The activities you want to be engaged in at this stage are all outward-facing.

- Recruiting in front of large groups of people
- Looking for new employees
- Telling your story in public and private forums
- Doing your guerrilla marketing
- Going to networking events to meet potential new clients
- Talking to the media
- Talking to potential investors

Leverage your energy in a good way by being the outward face of the company, so people feel your energy and buzz.

If you spend lots of money when you are both optimistic and uninformed, at some point you're going to cross the curve and see the real picture. Therefore, when you have feelings of manic energy . . .

- You don't want to be doing business planning.
- You don't want to be working on your budget.
- You don't want to be making buying decisions.
- You don't want to be making hiring decisions.
- You don't want to be doing your accounting or your book-keeping.

You don't want to be doing anything that requires you to think, plan, be logical, or make decisions. You just can't think straight and be calm enough for that!

Be aware that during the early stages of starting a company, or after you've landed a big PR coup such as a high-profile article about your company, advertising salespeople will start swarming around you. You will get phone calls from every crappy advertising salesperson that's ever walked the planet. The type who want to sell you pens with your company logo on them. These salespeople all subscribe to lists of business registrations. That's why they bombard all new businesses. They know that you're full of Uninformed Optimism, and they'll tell you how awesome your business is going to be, and that you should buy all this great advertising. And guess what happens? You come around the corner and you realize that you don't need it at all!

So remember that when you're in the first stage of the Transition Curve, you should spend time on anything that's outward facing and not make any buying, hiring, planning, or budgeting decisions.

Stage 2: Informed Pessimism

You've got more information now. You're not as excited as you once were. Coffee is helpful in getting you started on your day. You are worrying at times. You aren't depressed or really scared, but you're somewhere in between scared and excited. You're just a little bit pessimistic now.

The great thing with this stage is that it prevents you from making careless mistakes based on overly optimistic thinking. You've rounded the corner and have uttered the words, "Oh shit!" And unlike during Uninformed Optimism, at this stage you don't want to be talking to the media.

When you're experiencing Informed Pessimism and starting to feel that sense of nervousness that you *will* feel, that's when you want to start doing some planning—and some budgeting too. When you're nervous, you'll make better and tougher hiring decisions. You're going to be a lot more critical and discerning when you're interviewing prospective employees, and you'll be making sure that these people have really done what they say they've done and not just learned it in a textbook.

When you're in the Informed Pessimism stage you should be doing things like

- Planning the next phase of your growth
- Doing strategic planning on how to make your future unroll

- Budgeting
- Purchasing things like advertising (You'll be careful with where you spend your money and how much you spend, and you won't overbuy advertising based on potentially exuberant sales forecasts.)

Likewise, there are things you should avoid doing during this stage.

- Talking to the media or at speaking events
- Working in roles where being excited would help you get a better result (Wait until things turn around emotionally for you.)

Stage 3: Crisis of Meaning

This is a scary stage, and it can feel like you're standing on the edge of a building about to jump. It will feel like all the odds are stacked against you and that everything is going wrong. It will be hard to get out of bed in the morning. Sleeping at night will be close to impossible due to worries and fear. You'll feel like you're paralyzed and can do little more than perhaps clean your filing cabinet drawers successfully.

You definitely do *not* want to be talking to the media or potential employees or to be having team meetings when you're feeling like this.

When you start feeling yourself sliding into this Crisis of Meaning stage, you really do have to reach out for help. Don't wait until you're out on a ledge to call from your cell phone and say, "Hi, I'm getting ready to jump. Can you help me?" They won't even be able to get to you in time!

We all need to understand the feelings we're having as we move down the roller coaster. For women entrepreneurs, this can be a little easier since they know how to tap into that emotional intelligence and intuition from years of practice, and, frankly, it's more socially acceptable for them to do so. They're also more likely to talk to others about their feelings, whereas guys tend to think through stuff silently from our little caves. The bottom line? We all need to listen to our bodies and brains more.

That anxious feeling in your gut is a chemical reaction that your brain is triggering. Realize that your body is saying, "Slow down." This is the time to call on your friends, business advisers, banker, accountant, and even people you went to school with—anyone who can lend an ear—and ask them for guidance. Call on organizations like Accelerator, Entrepreneurs' Organization, or Young Presidents' Organization and say, "I'm feeling stressed, worried, and nervous. I'm not sure what to do or where to turn next. Help!"

Some of the best experiences I've had in business occurred during my first few years as 1-800-GOT-JUNK?'s COO. Founder Brian Scudamore and I would grab each other to go for walks when we noticed the other person was stressed. (We also did this when we noticed one of us was manic, too.) We'd just go for a long slow stroll around the building, with no objective in mind other than returning, eventually, to the front door. We wanted to just be there for each other personally through the stressful times of the business or life. We recognized that these stages were dangerous and wanted to be there for each other before things really got rough. We just helped each other calm down, and it never felt as lonely as it could have.

When you're moving toward Crisis of Meaning, you need to be able to communicate. Say, "Hey, I'm feeling stressed, terrified, completely anxious." And don't feel ashamed of it; every single business owner out there goes through this stuff. I promise!

So, as it turns out, being an entrepreneur is perfect if you've got attention deficit disorder or manic depression. Not to say you can't be an entrepreneur if you don't have one of these diseases, but darn it, it seems to be a great help! (I'm only half-serious, but leverage it if you have it.)

Again, support at this stage is key. You really need to be turning to and getting advice and encouragement from your support group: your church, your neighbors, your friends, your spouse, your family—anyone you can turn to so that you avoid this bottoming-out point. Be sure to let your significant other know about all five stages of the Transition Curve so he or she can keep you from "hitting the wall."

When you're at this stage you should do things like

- Cleaning your filing cabinet drawers—seriously. Doing a few little things can often perk you up.

- Reaching out to your support groups—friends, family, church, industry-related organizations. Ask them for help or advice, or to just lend an ear.
- Establishing your top five daily tasks and only working on the most important items each day
- Taking breaks and going for walks; exercising, meditating; spending time outdoors
- Having a drink: *one*, not many
- Writing lists—about your strengths, about what you love (Make lists that, when you reread them, will help rebuild your confidence.)
- Realizing that many others have been in this exact same place and usually have turned the corner just like you will
- Remembering the mantra of "The Little Engine That Could": "I think I can, I think I can." (It takes time, but you will turn the corner.)
- Getting introspective if it helps. What brought you to this point? How can you avoid it next time?
- Seeking advice from a professional or mentor who has been through it
- Doing anything that brings your energy up
- Going back to religion or finding some other spiritual foundation that will put your feet firmly on the ground
- Going to the movies. Just a complete distraction; two hours of escapism.
- Playing with your dog
- Reading an inspirational book

On the other hand, you should avoid doing things like

- Talking to others who are depressed! Misery loves company, but it doesn't make anyone feel better
- Talking to others who are "half empty" types; they'll only bring you down
- Taking advice from "all in" Vegas poker types
- Trying to "rally the troops" (your employees, the media)
- Taking more than one drink

- Thinking that you can handle it all on your own. You can't.
- Trying to learn more. Reading books and magazines about how to be successful or how to grow your company will only make you feel worse about your current situation

Here's a great question about this stage I received during one of my many speaking events:

> When you reach the Crisis of Meaning, how do you know whether you should Crash and Burn it, or persevere and continue?

First off, knowing what to do is different for everyone. Start by asking yourself: have I got the bandwidth, the people, the time, and the resources to get myself through this rough patch? Once you're able to really de-stress and get some support, you'll be able to look at that, because the last thing you want to do is keep trying to get through that window only to run out of cash six weeks later. You would have been better off stopping, keeping the cash, and spending it on the next business deal.

If you were really able to get hyper-focused, could you get through the curve? And then if you could, do you want to get back on it or would you prefer another ride instead? Is this a business that you really want to continue running? Your gut is going to tell you whether you really want to pull through it.

Stage 4: Crash and Burn

I won't really waste any time explaining this stage or what to do here; if you slide off the curve here, it really is over. The company is done, and so are you in the role of leader. My world is helping entrepreneurs *grow*, not helping them go bankrupt. So on we go . . .

Stage 5: Informed Optimism (or Hopeful Realization)

This last stage is much like the moment when the Little Engine That Could turned the corner and realized "he did" and "knew he would."

You'll start feeling energized again. And you'll start to feel momentum working in your favor again. You'll also have a lot more insight and experiential learning to draw from. You'll realize you have more competence and confidence than before, and everything will start to go your way. This would be the ideal stage to always be at. However, you won't be at this stage forever. More realistically, when you get here it just means you're getting ready to ride the roller coaster again.

Once you've gone through that bottom part of the curve, including the Crash and Burn stage, and you're coming out at the other side to Informed Optimism, you'll feel something click into place, just like when you're on a physical roller coaster. You'll feel that jerk as the chain grabs hold and the car comes to a stop. You have that sigh of relief as you realize you are okay, and now you've got the optimism that you'll need to start going up again. Just before that next ascent, you're more hopeful.

I've also heard this stage called Hopeful Realization. "I think I can, I think I can" turns into "I *knew* I could." You have to be really careful at this stage to not think that you made it on your own and thus pull away from your mentors and support groups. You might just slide backward off the track later and need them again.

On a real-life roller coaster, you can eventually get off. On the roller-coaster ride of entrepreneurship, you can't. The roller coaster just keeps on going over and over again.

MACRO AND MICRO CURVES

We talked about the macro curve that you're going to be going through; be aware that at each of the stages of the curve, you're going to face a lot of small micro curves as well. You could be about to reach the absolute height of Uninformed Optimism and get pulled down at just that instant. Or you could be at the exact bottom of Crisis of Meaning and some little "up" makes you feel good. These little micro curves happen all the time along the bigger macro curve.

My friend Mark called me one day and he was really excited. His business was opening the next week, and he said, "Cammy, I just hired three amazing employees."

"Mark, that's awesome," I said. "But you had only budgeted for one!"

"Oh shit! That's right."

Here was a person who was really excited he had hired three people, and when I reminded him he needed just one, he came back down to earth.

Mark called me about two days later all excited again. "Guess what? Two of them quit!"

You're going to have those little ups and downs, and then those big ups and downs. Be prepared for them and ride them out. And try to enjoy the ride along the Transition Curve roller coaster as much as you can.

Transition Curve

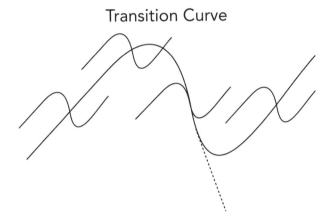

Remember, when riding a roller coaster, you have two choices: you can either hold on for dear life and scream, or you can wave your arms in the air and laugh. Either way, you are still riding the roller coaster. It's exactly the same when it comes to the Transition Curve. It's a certainty: you are going to ride it. Enjoy it as much as you can.

CHAPTER 13

PERSONAL PRODUCTIVITY

"It is not enough to be busy; so are the ants. The question is: What are we busy about?"
—Henry David Thoreau

Are you struggling to stay on task? Do you often feel like you are jumping from here to there and back again, only to forget where "here" was? The good news is that *you are not alone*. The bad news is: if you don't fix it, you *will* be alone (with a struggling business). This chapter has a ton of tactics you can and should use to help you and your company get more of the right stuff done.

Tom Peters, the author of *In Search of Excellence*, used to say that you need to be a "monomaniac with a mission." My first mentor, Greig Clark, recently told me that real leadership is saying no instead of yes. Saying no will provide more focus than saying yes to yet another project.

Multitasking may make you *feel* busy, but it doesn't *drive results*. It's impossible to get real results while doing two things at once. As I'm writing this section of the book, I am sitting in a very quiet room at Nita Lake Lodge at Whistler. No people around. No music. No phone or email. Just me tapping away on my laptop with the snow falling around me and a fireplace nearby. A perfect environment for focusing. Whatever type of environment you need to focus, find it and utilize it. Your productivity will improve and so will the quality of your work. Try turning off your cell phone, shutting down email, and focusing on projects for a little bit each day. You'll be amazed what you get done.

FOCUS DAYS

When building 1-800-GOT-JUNK?, I would often take "Focus Days" by myself or with Brian Scudamore, the founder and CEO. We'd put our feet up and work in silence without distractions from others or email. We'd take Focus Days once or twice a month.

No matter what business you operate, having Focus Days to get stuff accomplished can be extremely helpful. Take the time each month or every quarter to slow down, sit quietly, and obsess about the future. It always helped in reaching more thoughtful decisions about the present and future of the business.

During Focus Days, it's good to think about some of the following issues:

- Where in your business could you be focusing more?
- Who could you be building relationships with, whether inside or outside of the company?
- Who are your biggest clients?
- How could you get more business from them?

Are you taking some time to really focus, without the trappings of day-to-day busyness distracting you (laptop, email, phone)? I strongly urge you to think about taking a Focus Day (or a few) to disconnect from the rest of the world and be alone with yourself and your thoughts.

TIME MANAGEMENT

Time management isn't about just getting more things done. It's about focusing your efforts to get the more important things done, in less time. It's as simple as that. The amount of time and money you'll save with proper time management will astound you.

There are an infinite number of demands on your time and attention. Many problems and tasks are new and can't be planned for; many are urgent and thrown at you by coworkers. The consequences of using your time effectively or ineffectively are huge.

Time management is a habit that begins with goal setting. Without goals, you're merely putting lists of "stuff" on your plate.

Before the start of each week, month, or quarter, write down all of the goals you want to achieve during that period of time. Thirty minutes of focusing will allow you to really plan what goals you want to hit and how you want to hit them. Always think in advance, but be focused on *now*.

The hardest part of time management is sticking to your plan. The second hardest part is knowing when to change part of the plan so that you can hit your goals.

Getting Started with Time Management

Getting started with time management does require some planning, but once you familiarize yourself with the process, it will become second nature to you. Here is a simple outline for how you can take all the stuff on your plate and start getting more of the impactful stuff done, and relieving some of the stress you feel too.

1. List activities.

List everything that you have to do in the time frame for which you're planning. Do a full brain-dump. Don't miss a thing.

2. Prioritize the items in the list.

I first read this little story about ten years ago (as told by Frank L. Tibolt, though it had circulated in the business world for many decades before that and was popularized by Napoleon Hill's *Think and Grow Rich*). It has had a profound impact on helping me become more accomplished; it simplifies everything about the way you approach projects on a daily basis.

> One day a management consultant, Ivy Lee, called on Charles M. Schwab of the Bethlehem Steel Company. Lee briefly outlined his firm's services, ending with the statement: "With our service, you'll know how to manage better."
>
> The indignant Schwab said, "I'm not managing as well now as I know how. *What we need around here is not more 'knowing' but*

more doing; not 'knowledge,' but action; if you can give us some-thing to pep us up to do the things we *already know* we ought to do, I'll gladly listen to you and pay you anything you ask."

"Fine," said Lee. "I can give you something in twenty minutes that will step up your action and doing at least 50 percent."

"Okay," said Schwab. "I have just about that much time before I must leave to catch a train. What's your idea?"

Lee pulled a blank 3" x 5" note sheet out of his pocket, handed it to Schwab and said: "Write on this sheet the six most important tasks you have to do tomorrow." That took about three minutes. The beauty of using a small piece of paper is that you have to be concise.

"Now," said Lee, "number them in the order of their impor-tance." Five more minutes passed.

"Now," said Lee, "put this sheet in your pocket and the first thing tomorrow morning, look at item one and start working on it. Pull the sheet out of your pocket every fifteen minutes and look at item one until it is finished. Then tackle item two in the same way, then item three. Do this until quitting time. Don't be concerned if you only finished two or three, or even if you only finish one item. You'll be working on the important ones. The others can wait. If you can't finish them all by this method, you couldn't with another method either, and without some system you'd probably not even decide which are most important."

He went on, "Spend the last five minutes of every working day making out a 'must do' list for the next day's tasks. After you've convinced yourself of the worth of this system, have your men try it. Try it out as long as you wish and then send me a check for what *you* think it's worth."

The whole interview lasted about twenty-five minutes. In two weeks, Schwab sent Lee a check for $25,000—a thousand dollars a minute. He added a note saying the lesson was the most profit-able he had ever learned. Did it work? In five years it turned the unknown Bethlehem Steel Company into the biggest independent steel producer in the world, and made Schwab a hundred-million-dollar fortune, and the best-known steel man alive at that time.

This story has been rewritten in many books and blogs, but this version is the one with which I'm most familiar. The beauty of it is that it outlines one of the simplest tools for setting goals that I've ever encountered. I've found it so helpful in keeping me on task and on time that, in addition to using the top-six method on a daily basis, I use the same concept to stay focused on quarterly, monthly, and weekly goals, too. Although the original story may involve drafting up your top six goals each day, I use variations on the number—top five or top three—depending on the area of business with which I'm working. The thinking is simple: the lower the number, the more focus I hope to impart. No matter which number you use, or which version of the story you've read, this is pretty darn close to what happened. Doing your top five daily allows you to do a few of the critical things well, instead of working on a bunch of random tasks. (And if this system helps your company, you're welcome to send me a check one day to say thank you!)

Now to expand the top-five concept a little bit. After you've listed your activities, split them into A and B priorities. The letter A is usually reserved for items that will help you hit your goals. The letter B is for items that should get done if possible. Once you've done this, rank each A item according to importance: A1, A2, and so on. Then repeat this process with the Bs.

Once you are done, start putting each of the activities into your calendar with specific times you'll do them. For instance: *10:00–11:00: Interview Customer Support Rep (A1)*.

Remember when you're putting the As and then the Bs into your calendar to be specific with times and to leave time for such interruptions as emails and phone calls, because you *will* get them. You'll need the buffer time to allow you to stay on track.

The hardest part is sticking to the plan. We've all caught ourselves working on low-priority tasks such as cleaning out our desk drawers or checking email instead of working on critical projects. If you're looking for help in this area, there is a new fantastic application to assist you and your employees in focusing on your top five tasks; it's called Teamly (www.Teamly.com), and I'm now an advisor and investor in the company.

The second hardest part is knowing when to modify your plan. For example, maybe it's more important to continue an A-priority call and run over time than to end on time to start a B-priority item you've already scheduled. An A task should always take priority over a B task. And lower numbers, such as A3, have priority over higher ones, like A7.

Remember: plan your work and work your plan. I find that telling at least one other person what you are going to get done in a day will help you stay focused on doing it.

3. Review often.

Review your progress often, typically daily and weekly. Are you hitting your goals? Have all A priorities been completed? Reviewing is the best time to transfer uncompleted Bs to a new day.

4. Analyze your performance.

Did you take too long to do any of the tasks? If so, why? Were they worth doing? Is there anything you can do to better manage your time tomorrow?

Finding Your Unique Ability

Years ago, I took a course by Dan Sullivan called "Strategic Coach," during which he taught something he called "unique ability." Dan now also has a book out by the same name. My unique ability turned out to be that I use quick, intuitive ideas to help entrepreneurs reverse engineer their dreams. In a perfect world, I would outsource, delegate, or stop doing anything other than those tasks that utilize my unique ability.

Here's how Dan Sullivan defines "unique ability" in his Strategic Coach program: "First, it is a superior ability that other people notice and value; second, we love doing it and want to do it as much as possible; third, it is energizing both for us and others around us; and, fourth, we keep getting better, never running out of possibilities for further improvement."

In order to truly focus, use this simple exercise to help you start working only on items that draw on your unique ability:

Make a list in Excel of everything you do daily and weekly. I like to pretend someone took a video of me working all day for a month, and I imagine the movie while I write everything down.

Now put all of those items in column one of the spreadsheet.

In column two, put one of these four letters describing your skill level related to the task:

I = Incompetent—You're terrible at it.

C = Competent—You're okay at it.

E = Excellent—You're awesome at it (but you don't love it).

U = Unique Ability—Dan's definition (given in the preceding paragraph).

In column three, put the hourly wage you'd be willing to pay someone to do that task as a full-time job.

Then begin quickly delegating, stopping, or outsourcing the lowest-paying tasks and the tasks on which you gave yourself a C or I rating.

This simple system will help you quickly become more focused on doing exactly what you need to do to grow your company and love doing it. Imagine if you had everyone in your company working strictly on areas that warranted the wage you were paying them, or on tasks on which both they and you would rate them E or U.

TIPS FOR STAYING FOCUSED

Over the years, I've kept an updated list of tips on how to stay focused gathered from various places. Every six months I'll come across it and reread it. It always gives me a little boost of focus and helps me get more done. Hopefully some of these ideas will help you and your team focus more too.

Breathe. During her talk, the great speaker Victoria Labalme quoted the famous mime Marcel Marceau, under whom she had studied: "Breathe, breathe." And it's amazing how just slowing down to breathe like they do in yoga really helps the brain focus.

Compress Time. Pretend you have just two hours a day to work. What three to five things would you do during those two hours each day? Once you know what those are, delegate or stop doing everything else that you currently do and start doing only those three to five things all day, every day.

Eat Something! It's hard to concentrate when your tummy is rumbling, so have a light snack before you settle in to work on your top priorities. Not only will you avoid the "When is lunch?" thoughts, but a healthy snack will also give you more energy and help you think better. Cathy Stucker gave me this piece of advice, and it's one I always remember.

Get Out of Email. Email is one of the worst time-wasters ever. Start your day working on one of your top five projects for the day. Check email at 4:00 PM; no earlier. It can wait. As soon as you start checking email, the temptation will be to get sucked into it, draining your productivity. Years ago, I sent all eight of my direct reports the same email at 9:00 AM: "Don't tell anyone, but come find me in the boardroom right away." I then walked calmly to the boardroom. Within three minutes, six of my eight reports were in the boardroom. The other two were there by the five-minute mark. It quickly showed them and me how little they were focused on the critical projects and how distracted they could be with emails. I've even tried this with CEOs whom I mentor and coach. Most of them call me instantly. A few are awesome and don't call until the following day, saying, "Sorry I didn't get to you sooner, but I'm doing what you told me and not checking email." Exactly what I wanted. You may have a couple of people in your office who need to be watching the inbox carefully, but surely not everyone in your company needs to be stuck in it.

Let Fear Guide You. Nothing helps you focus quite like fear. Harness it. And by this I mean rational fear and competition, not paranoia.

Minimize Distractions. "A messy desk is a messy mind." The more clutter you have on the desk, in the workstation, and on the walls around you, the more distracted you are. Keeping a clean work area will help you focus.

Put Your Headphones On. Put 'em on, put on some great tunes, and crank out your work. I actually can be hyper-productive listening to a genre of music called psy-trance. It gets every ounce of me pumped up and focused. Find your tunes and get listening.

Reward Yourself. Break your projects into smaller, more achievable parts. Upon completing each part, give yourself a reward—like a night out. I don't allow myself a glass of wine with dinner unless I have the next day's top five tasks in writing.

Set Timers. It may seem crazy, but it works. You can use a simple timer. Set it for thirty minutes and then focus on *one thing* until the thirty minutes are up.

Slay the Dragon. Each day, identify the big ugly task you must complete. Start with it first. Once you have the thing you are dreading out of the way, the rest looks easy. It also gives you a boost of confidence.

Tell Two Others. Tell two to three people something that you are going to do and when you will have it done by. Be very specific about the date and what the outcome will be. When doing this with your employees, get them to tell you the key projects they will have done that day too. This is a great example of where a coach can truly help an entrepreneur.

Turn Off the Damn "Ding." Turn off notifications on all your devices. The last thing you want while you're trying to focus is something telling you that your attention is required elsewhere. Remember the old AOL "You've got mail!" announcement? Evil. But it's been replaced with a million other dings, pings, and pop-ups. You don't need it when you're trying to be productive.

Write 'Em Down. Know that saying "out of sight, out of mind"? It applies to the items on your daily To Do list too, so put your weekly and daily lists on a whiteboard, flip chart, or even a Post-it note on your monitor. I use an app called "Stickies" on my Mac. Seeing your key projects in front of you all day will force you to focus.

—

No matter how productive you are, you can't achieve your Painted Picture alone. In addition to mastering efficient work habits, you will also have to reach out to others if you really want to double the size of your company in three years. This may be the hardest thing you have to do: go out and find help before you need it. Let's take a look at how a board of advisers can help you reach your growth goal.

CHAPTER 14

BOARD OF ADVISERS

"I have found the best way to give advice to your children is to find out what they want and then advise them to do it."
—Harry S. Truman

I was on a flight home from a Berkshire Hathaway shareholders' meeting in Omaha, Nebraska, after having spoken to a large group of entrepreneurs from Entrepreneurs' Organization who were also in town for the meeting. While there, I was thinking about the difference between a board of directors and a board of advisers. What struck me was how entirely different their roles are, and how so many entrepreneurs are missing out by not assembling a board of advisers for their company.

Most entrepreneurs think these boards are expensive items only for big companies. This is not true. If you are smart, you can put together a board of advisers that will cost you little but result in big rewards for you and your company. A board of advisers can keep you focused and keep your company on track.

During the past ten years, I've been both an internal and an external member of the board of advisers for a couple of companies. In my prior role as COO of 1-800-GOT-JUNK?, I was an internal board member attending and helping to lead the meetings for close to seven years. I was also a board member at Nurse Next Door, a Canadian franchisor of at-home senior care, for three years. Through these experiences, I've learned the keys to creating a high-performing board.

It starts with understanding that the role of the board is to advise and help hold the CEO and leadership of a company accountable. One critical distinction between a board of advisers and a board of directors is that the former cannot fire the CEO, while the latter can. The board of advisers can be comprised of any mix of internal and external members the CEO wants. Essentially, the board is there to help the CEO.

SELECTING BOARD MEMBERS

After you realize you need a board, the next critical step is selecting the right people to serve on it. Without the right people, your board of advisers will never deliver its full value.

In my opinion, you're looking for company-builders to serve on your board, not lawyers and accountants. Too many people make the mistake of putting lawyers and accountants on the board. I call this a mistake because you can easily pay such professionals for their advice, and their advice, due to the nature of their professions, is frequently more risk-averse than a growing company needs it to be. With lawyers and accountants on your board, you also tend to get advice aligned with why you *shouldn't* do things rather than how you might be able to do them. Entrepreneurship is inherently a risky business. That's not going to appeal to lawyers and accountants, and in the end, their reluctance may stifle your growth.

You want to stack your board with people who are not only experts in niches such as marketing, advertising, HR, strategic alliances, multi-unit franchising, or international business, but who have also helped build companies in the past at a leadership level. You want people who live in or *very* close to your city, too, so that scheduling meetings is easier. Lastly, you want a three- to five-year commitment from them since you'll learn more as they get deeper into the psyche of the company.

It's critical to get people on the board who have *built* companies, not just *run* them. Getting people involved who have led large companies is also critical as you become a professional organization with complex structures and strategic planning issues that you didn't have in the earlier growth phases.

In finding your key board members, you are looking for people who want to help you and aren't just doing it for the money. Typically, board members get paid $500 to $2,000 per meeting. Occasionally, they are offered a small annual retainer. There is no need to give equity or options unless the members are making key introductions for you or if you are using their name and reputation to build your company's credibility.

PREPARATION

In 1994, I did a speaking event called "The 6 Ps," which were "Proper Preparation Prevents Piss-Poor Performance." My own Golden Rule is as sound today as it was back in '94, especially when it comes to working with a board of advisers.

To fully prepare your board of advisers, it is critical that you provide them with your Painted Picture. It is critical that the board and the company as a whole focus on your Painted Picture—you want the board to focus on the future, not where the company is today. Too often I see board members get embroiled in tactical, day-to-day, or urgent matters when their time would have been better spent discussing the balance sheet, how they intend to facilitate cash flow growth, or how they'd handle things like massive currency fluctuations, recessions, continued hyper-growth, etc. One of the board's goals should be to stay ahead of the vision of the company, or, worst case, keep up with it.

Once you are sure the board understands your Painted Picture, it's your and your team's job to ensure that the board receives a package of materials that will bring them up to speed well in advance of the meeting (at least one week). Yes, I know you're busy, but your advisers are busy too. You want to give them lots of advance notice about the issues you'll be talking about at the meeting. By giving your board members this report, you'll give them more time to prepare, which ultimately helps you and your business.

Ideally, the report should be brief and contain updates on

- The company's achievements since the last meeting
- The areas in which the company is struggling
- Any key metrics
- Financial statements showing key ratios and performance ver-

sus budget, including previous quarter and year performance (It's important that you trust your board implicitly. And giving them the full set of financial statements is key. They'll uncover precious gems that no one else sees; not only will they have the numbers in front of them, but they also have the benefit of all the confidential discussions they've had with you, which will cause some numbers to jump out at them when other people wouldn't have noticed a thing.)

- Key decisions the company may be facing in the coming quarter and year
- The Painted Picture, as an ongoing reminder of what's being built

The board's prep package should also focus on

- Facts, as well as feelings various leadership team members have regarding the company
- Specifics, not generalizations
- The absolute truth. If there are stressors that exist between members of the leadership team, then those underlying facts must be revealed to the board so they can help you. As soon as a leadership team is worried that the board members might "think less of them" if some fact is brought into the open, trust begins to erode and the advice the board gives is never as informed as it could have and should have been.

RUNNING THE MEETING

Meetings should be held four to six times a year, and each one should be roughly three to four hours in length. The meetings should cover questions on the prep packages without just restating what the board members have already read. The prep package is meant to be *preparation reading*, not content to be rehashed later.

Who should attend these meetings? The CEO and key leaders. Often I would have a VP come to the board meeting, present his or her six-month plan, get hammered by the board, and leave. This always turned out to be a hugely valuable growing experience for the VP and for the company.

After roughly one hour, the meeting should shift into creative discussion, insight gathering, and debate around two to three critical areas the company is working on. If the meeting is run properly, it should be less like a presentation and more like a group discussion. Challenge each other in a constructive way in order to gain the best possible insights and a sound consensus.

Reviewing your financial statements is also worthwhile at these meetings because board members tend to ask the "dumb" questions, which opens leadership's eyes to areas of opportunity or concern that may not have jumped out at them when they reviewed the statements themselves.

Last, each member should be adding to all topics and not just giving advice from his or her area of specialty. You want everyone's experiences and questions on all topics to be discussed.

ACCOUNTABILITY

The highest-performing companies are those that do what they said they'll do at board meetings, and the highest-performing boards are those of companies that allow all fears, ideas, and frustrations to be disclosed to the board, rather than giving them only good news. Transparency is crucial to a functional and productive board.

Keep detailed notes of what each member of the leadership team commits to during the board discussion. See to it that those commitments get kept and that you deliver on your promises between board meetings. You should never placate members by agreeing to "look into" an issue or "confront" some brutal fact. If you mean what you say and say what you mean, then the board will see that their advice is being heeded, and they'll work hard to give you even better advice moving forward. If a board is feeling merely placated, then rest assured they'll stop caring about the advice they give.

OTHER IMPORTANT SOURCES OF OUTSIDE ADVICE

In addition to your board of advisers, you will need to tap into a variety of different sources of information. If you do not continue expanding your leadership abilities, you will never be able to achieve the growth you desire. As your company doubles its size, you too must grow as a leader.

Professional Learning Organizations

There are many organizations across the globe that support and foster entrepreneurial growth. Organizations such as Young Presidents' Organization (YPO), Entrepreneurs' Organization (EO), and Vistage all have forum programs. Members join these groups (called "forums") of eight to twelve other noncompeting entrepreneurs who then meet monthly in a confidential setting to assist each other in growing their companies. All entrepreneurs and CEOs or presidents of companies should look into and seriously consider joining one of these organizations. They provide invaluable board-like learning, mentoring, and accountability. My years in an EO forum and as a member of the Vancouver chapter of the Entrepreneurs' Organization provided a quantum leap in my business learning.

Coaches and Mentors

I've found that the highest-performing leaders and companies are the ones that reach out to many outside experts for advice in addition to having a board of advisers. As humans, we're hardwired to help each other. When people reach out to us for advice, it makes us feel good. I'm not old or bored enough to be on traditional boards, but advisory boards are awesome and another great way I help entrepreneurs make their dreams happen.

I've been coaching entrepreneurs for more than twenty years now and have helped many establish and execute their strategic plans. I've also shown them easy-to-implement, scalable systems to help them grow their companies. Most high-ranking CEOs have coaches or mentors, even if they never talk about them. Successful people learn from other successful people, which is why I recommend that you try getting one for your company. You'll wonder how you survived without one.

Ad Hoc Mentors

For years I've been connecting with people at conferences, via casual introductions and through the general course of business. In all of these interactions, I take note of which individuals are sharp. When I meet them, I also make sure to note what their strengths are and how they can perhaps be of help to me in the future. Then, when I head back to the office, or oftentimes on flights, I'll enter their contact information into my computer, and in the notes field, I'll write the word "mentor" and also jot down a few key areas where they are strong: for example, "mentor marketing," "YPO," "employee engagement," and so on. The idea behind building this database is to not only accumulate names but also to build relationships with them over time so I can turn to them for mentoring when I need it. I have a friend who calls his list of contacts his "MBA," or "mentor board of advisers."

It's been my good fortune to be wise enough to connect with the real smart people and do what they tell me throughout my life. In addition to the lists I've built in my contacts on my laptop, I've also built a strong list of connections on Facebook, LinkedIn, and Twitter, and I reach out to those often as well. You don't need a formal board of advisers for yourself, just a long list of people you've met over the years who you can start calling on. Start your list now. You'll find that advisers will not only help you focus on growing your company but will also help you focus on improving your quality of life.

CHAPTER 15

WORK-LIFE BALANCE

"Mens sana in corpore sano"
—translated from Latin as "a healthy mind in a healthy body"

When you created your Painted Picture, you included personal goals about how you wish to live as your company grows. Too often, entrepreneurs forget these personal goals as they strive to attain their business goals. Remember that you must focus on every part of your Painted Picture. If you are not able to achieve your personal goals, you will not be able to achieve your professional goals, and you will run a high risk of burning out as your company moves up the growth curve.

That's why it is essential that you get a life. Seriously. Recently, a would-be entrepreneur told me he was working constantly and struggled to read books for fun. I threw down the gauntlet and told him he'd never be a successful entrepreneur until he figured out how to get a life. I told him to read the book *Endurance*, Alfred Lansing's true-life account of Ernest Shackleton's fateful voyage to the Antarctic. And I told him not to contact me until he'd finished it. The great thing is, I knew he'd read it that week, and I know he'll be successful in finding balance in this world.

I'm a big believer that a focus on the "life" part of work-life balance provides a virtuous circle in which improving your quality of life will also improve you professionally. That is to say, the best way to become a more productive worker is to focus more on the things outside of work that invigorate and recharge you, as this will positively impact the time you are spending at work.

I'm not an expert in work-life balance, but through crashing twice, and hard, I've come to learn a few things about it. I crashed harder than I'd wish on anyone else, so I try to help others as best I can. Here are some of my favorite tips for finding a healthy work-life balance.

1. **Work hard, play hard**. Sure, we've all heard this saying, but rarely do we live it. Nowadays, people do a lot of hard work, but when it comes time to fulfill the other end of the obligation, we give up, bringing our laptops, cell phones, and other "work" items into our "play time." And from what I recall as a kid, playing hard didn't include toting along our homework, or in the modern world, our iPhone or Black-Berry. We just played—played until we dropped from laughing so hard. Played until we dropped from exhaustion and slept like babies. It's time to return to that kind of play, not just for your individual sanity but for the sake of those who care about you.

2. **Build a support network**. I'm not sure why it's so common, but entrepreneurs tend to overwhelm themselves with guilt for not working around the clock. Often our non–business owner friends wonder why we work so hard, or why we can't ever "disconnect." Start building a network of people in your support system who understand your passion and don't make you feel guilty about chasing it, but who will also hold you accountable for spending time on the other parts of your life.

3. **Don't say it; do it**. Stop saying you want to do things. Stop saying you want to learn things. Stop saying you want to try things. Stop talking about your Bucket List and start crossing things off of it. I talked today via email with a friend in Boston, David Hauser. He'd just come back from a one-hour bike ride in the dead of winter with a fellow entrepreneur, Kris Kaplan. David and Kris aren't talking about it. *They're doing it.* Kris has become a maniacally focused athlete, and when he's not having fun, he's working, and hard. David has an annual pass to a go-kart racetrack—awesome. Still makes me laugh. Make a commitment to stop saying you're going to do something and go ahead and do it.

4. **Schedule family time**. Put family time in your calendar first and schedule everything else around it. I've always wanted to walk my kids to school. So, I do. Every morning I have a standing appointment from 8:45 to 9:15 to walk them to school. I book breakfasts, meetings,

and calls around that time. Sometimes, I need to use that spot. But I'll bet I walk my kids to school more often than you do. And I'll remember it more than the meeting I could have had.

5. **Pre-book kids' events**. Ask for your kids' school calendar in September like I do, and book "off time" on all the dates your kids are off too. Those "professional development days" that teachers get off seem to happen at random times, but they make great days to play with the kids. This is way better bonding time than simply going to the standard school play that we watch them in once a year. And by booking them off in your calendar months in advance you'll be assured of spending it with them.

6. **Stop the insanity of email**. Only check email twice a day. I'm still not great at this but I'm getting better. Stop the insanity of checking email first thing every day. Yes, email is great. Yes, email helps us. However, the people getting the most done are not checking email first thing in the morning, nor are they checking email throughout the day. You've heard this dozens of times, so why are you still choosing to be one of the unproductive ones? If you have the type of company where replying to customer inquiries quickly potentially means losing or winning the deal, then find a way to have one person be responsible for checking email frequently. Surely not everyone in your company has to be glued to his or her inbox.

7. **Look in the rearview mirror**. I don't need to push many entrepreneurs to set goals. They do that naturally. I do, however, need to push them to see how far they've come. A great way to feel good about yourself and to relax a bit at the end of each week is to review everything you accomplished that week. Write down a list of the top five things you accomplished and let it sink in. Allow yourself to feel good about what you got done before you set next week's tasks. If you're always focused on the horizon you'll never relax. Look in the rearview mirror to see how far you've come.

8. **Exercise often**. Enough said.

9. **Turn off the lights**. Don't work at night or on weekends. You'll never get it all done. Don't try. It's about working smarter, not longer. It's

about outsourcing and moving repetitive tasks offshore, not working harder. It's about being focused, not working seventeen-hour days. Trust me, I've tried both. Make a list of every task you do, and get someone else to do the stuff you don't have time for.

10. **Don't watch the clock**. Watch the results, not the clock. Some of the most productive people work fewer hours, but they also do the most focused work. I used to make jokes about bankers' hours only to see how it punished those who got into the office early, worked hard, and left at a normal hour to play sports. I had it backward. Many of those being praised for staying late actually showed up three hours later, worked with less focus, stayed late, got less done, and inspired no one because they had no balance in their lives.

11. **Hire people who play**. Look for athletes and hire people who play sports actively. Recruit for it. Look for team players. Look for those with athletic goals as adults. Those who wake up working hard will work hard in their jobs, too. Those who sit on the couch watching TV that makes them dumber will produce similar results at work.

FURTHER TIPS ON WORK-LIFE BALANCE

I went out to my vast network of connections on Twitter, Facebook, and LinkedIn and my blog subscribers to get ideas too. And I got some great ones. Here they are.

- It's not about balancing work and life. It's about paying respect to the individual relationships we cultivate: the relationship with self, with work, and (hopefully) with the person you get to put your cold feet up against at night.
- I turn my radio off and my cell phone off so I'm 100 percent present and in the moment with the kids for the fifteen-minute drive or walk to school.
- I not only get "me time," I also work to get one-on-one time with each of the kids. Even if it's an overnight trip somewhere with each of the kids.

- If you've got job flexibility, avoid rush hour traffic to and from work and travel during off-peak hours. Use that saved time with the kids, before they go to school or after they come home, or for exercise.

- Whatever you choose to make a priority, you will make happen! You also lead by example as your kids watch and learn. For example, choose stairs over escalators; choose walking instead of moving walkways at the airport. When I take an elevator I play a game where I do a squat (only when no one else is in the elevator with me!) and have to stay in that position till I get to whatever floor I've pressed.

- Travel with a skipping rope and tubing so you can exercise in your hotel room. In fifteen minutes of push-ups, abdominal crunches, and dips, you can get a very good workout without leaving your room. No need to travel with running shoes or worry about finding a gym. Watch CNN and exercise.

- First, I realize that balance is an illusion. Life is never in balance, so I work to manage the imbalances to ensure that critical issues are always taken care of (first things first), and then I work to optimize.

- I book blocks of time in our family calendar to take vacations before we even know where it is we will be going. I want to ensure we have no excuses of being too busy.

- Write out your priorities and think about which ones you are neglecting. Recently, my kids got very annoyed that I was constantly checking my iPhone, so I looked at my list and reminded myself that a priority was not to look at email while I was in their presence.

- Start the year by booking your holidays and time off in advance.

- I have a weekly half-day volunteer commitment. Forces me to spend some mid-week time not working.

- At work, I pretend I have no personal life. At home, I pretend I'm jobless. (*Grin*) Doing both forces me to be 100 percent present on whatever I'm doing or supposed to be doing.

- Pretend that your iPhone only works when the sun is up and not at all on weekends. Kids and spouses need to believe they are the most important part of your life.

- The iPhone is like a huge "presence" condom. It numbs the feeling.

- Do a Painted Picture for your family or personal life as well as your business. Work hard at making your family Painted Picture come true, just like you do your business one. Companies come and go. Family is forever. Paint the family's future together and enjoy the journey.

- I realized email and cell calls are never urgent. It dawned on me that nobody has ever called me to buy a million dollars of stuff. I only sell when I am doing the calling. So why am I thinking their emails or calls are so urgent?

- Ask women what they're doing—and do that. Women tend to get balance a lot more than men do. Learn from them. They get it. And they live it a lot better—or they sure try to.

—

If you are able to achieve a work-life balance, achieving the growth goals for your company will be much easier. More importantly, you will be able to enjoy the challenges of meeting your goals. Will you be able to double your personal happiness as you double the size of your company? Happiness is something that I can't guarantee. But I can guarantee that, with work-life balance as a priority, your quality of life will improve for both you and your family as you watch your company double in size over the next three years.

CHAPTER 16

IN SUMMARY

From my experience with College Pro Painters, from 1986 to 1988, to 1-800-GOT-JUNK?, from 2000 to 2007, and even Boyd Autobody between those two, from 1994 to 1998, I've seen how these systems can work incredibly well to grow companies. The hundreds of companies globally who continue to use these systems today after learning them from me prove this point even further.

With College Pro Painters my revenues doubled, and profits tripled in just two years. With 1-800-GOT-JUNK?, we averaged 100 percent revenue growth for six consecutive years. At Boyd Autobody, our franchise expansion allowed us to more than double the number of locations we had in one year, and triple the number of locations we had over three years. Our buying power, brand awareness, and profitability expanded exponentially as well.

The keys to this doubling were always the same.

Every company had a crystal clear vision of what was being built, and that vision was shared with everyone the company touched or employed.

Awesome people were recruited, hired, trained, and handcuffed. Culture was key. It was always about building something more than a business. And we knew that great people would make it happen.

It then came down to reverse engineering the future with simple backward scheduling applied to everything. Just like putting together a jigsaw puzzle.

To figure out how to do each of the projects that we'd need to grow, I would use R&D, which stood for Rip Off & Duplicate. So many great companies have already figured it all out; I'd just figure out who they were and do what they'd done before me.

One key to growth had always been doing it faster. Everything can be faster. Perfectionism and procrastination are killing companies. When you think you're going too fast, step on the gas.

Part of going faster was leverage. We realized that everything can be leveraged into something else. A PR angle, a newsletter, or a blog piece could be a starting point for something bigger. A meeting or new employee could lead to introductions to someone else. Once everyone knew what our vision of the future looked like, we could always leverage things into something else. One plus one always equaled five.

Last, but definitely not least, I learned to not take myself so F'n seriously. It's all a game. The businesses we build are there to give us and our employees great experiences and lives along the way, not just once we're done. I learned to have fun at work, and I used to say TGIM—"Thank God It's Monday"—because I loved building every business I worked on, and I still love coaching and mentoring CEOs today who feel the same way.

CHAPTER 17

LETTERS TO MYSELF

"Waste no more time arguing about what a good man should be. Be one."
—Marcus Aurelius

On leaving 1-800-GOT-JUNK?, after nearly seven years and being in the role of chief operating officer, I really wanted the lessons I had learned to sink in. So, over the period of the three months immediately following, I wrote for twenty minutes every day in a journal to capture what I'd learned. I wrote lists. I mind-mapped. I just wrote. These fifty-eight points are some of the key lessons I learned about myself during that period of reflecting. I still read my journal every few months to remind myself of these tips and to keep learning. I hope they help you too.

I wish I had received this advice as letters from my future self back when I was a sixteen-year-old entrepreneur starting out. It certainly would have been an easier ride.

1. **De-Stress**. De-stress daily & weekly. The residual stress builds up in me. I can feel it. The stress inside me definitely affects the team and me in negative ways. I react differently when it's building up in me.

2. **Slow Down, Do Less**. I'm way more effective when I work at about 80% of the manic speed I can get myself up to. If I booked fewer meetings back-to-back, if I used buffer time, if I spent more time in 1-on-1 interactions, I'd be much more productive. My intuitive leadership style is more effective when I'm not rushing around.

3. **Don't React**. I move too fast without thinking about the ripple effects of my actions or words. I make decisions too quickly without thinking about the effects on other departments or about whether we're

even ready for the large initiatives to happen. People think I'm shooting from the hip even when I'm not. I need to stop and try to clearly think about what I'm going to say before I say it.

4. **Boundaries.** Set them—I never did. I can't be all things to all people. I can't work 60-hour workweeks and be productive. I have to learn how to say no vs. taking everything on that others could easily do or that we could delay until another time. I can't "cover" for people. I tried covering for people's mental health issues, people who wanted to have more balance in their lives, people who didn't work as efficiently, etc. I would handle conflict situations that other people should have dealt with on their own. I worked overtime when team members couldn't sell or didn't want to work nights at social events, with suppliers or Franchise Partners. I have to stop checking email at night and just do all my work during the work hours of they day—instead of working two jobs' worth of hours.

5. **Mentor While You Work.** I watched two very senior team members mentoring people as they did their jobs. They would take their junior people into meetings and just let them watch them do their jobs. It was interesting to watch their team learn along the way. I used to just put my head down and work, but they were smarter and let their team watch them work so the team could learn at the same time. It was easier for the mentor to delegate faster to people who'd learned quicker.

6. **Get Money, Especially When You Don't Need It.** That's the time to make sure you get credit lines and financing in place—while your balance sheet is strong. When you need money, you have to be able to act. When you need money, no one will want to loan it to you. Even if you think you don't need it, you soon will. Keep increasing the amounts you have available to you as you grow. Systematically, every 6–12 months, keep getting all credit lines increased, and do it at a time when your business is financially strongest. Don't just grow using cash; leverage the cash you have to use multiple finance mechanisms.

7. **Seasonal Businesses Are Tough.** Cash flow is harder in a seasonal business. College Pro Painters did all of its revenues in just 4 months. 12 months of expenses and only 4 months of revenues. Makes it really

tough. The founder, Greig Clark, used to mortgage his house every winter to get us to spring revenues. Seasonal businesses amplify the bad times and promote sloppiness in good times.

8. **Don't Bring Problems Home**. Just be. My wife used to say she got leftover Cameron. That's because often when I got home, I'd be so exhausted I had nothing left to give. I need to put my problems in a box and leave them at work at the end of the day. They'll be there in the morning, and they'll always get worked out. Stewing about them overnight doesn't help.

9. **Running**. It's amazing for me. It relaxes me, helps me think, clarifies my mind, and quiets me. I always feel better and more confident not only during the run but afterward too.

10. **Confrontation**. My debates tended to be about arguing to be right instead of arguing to solve a problem. I'd let things get to me personally. I would at times feel like I was being attacked or criticized. I countered my insecurities by arguing, and it never helped.

11. **Listening**. When I am listening to a person's problems, I am a great listener. When I am in a meeting, I don't let other people speak; I keep cutting them off. I've learned to catch myself and to slow down my thinking. If I truly am listening to them I don't need to talk as much.

12. **Do As I Say**. I'm technically very intuitive in knowing how to grow a company. I move too fast to always "do" what I know works. I know that following systems helps ensure consistency and that those systems save time, but I often waste time or cause problems by not using them consistently.

13. **Conscious Stream of Thought**. I work great by pacing and thinking out loud. I often need people to let me run and write something down while I'm thinking verbally so we can discuss it later. At times I'll even change my mind as I'm talking and not even remember my original comments.

14. **Outcome Over Process**. Sometimes all the planning, tracking & details of the plan get in the way of getting things done. I'm very big on focusing on the outcome vs. the process to get us to the result faster (but

see point 12 for how it can also get in the way). Sometimes the process is necessary.

15. **The Secret.** It's just so much better to stay in a positive mind-set. I've learned how to recognize my stress and negative feelings and quickly switch them back to be positive again. Awareness of the negatives is okay, but focusing on them is bad. I shouldn't wear my emotions on my sleeve as much as I do.

16. **Intuition.** I have it. I am learning to trust it, to listen to it, to call on it.

17. **Negative Public Comments.** My role is to stay as a "cheerleader" and to stay positive. My role would have greater impact by cheering my team on rather than showing them where they need to improve. Especially publicly. I need to stay focused on raising the energy level of the group at all times. I need to ask myself every day, What did I do today to raise the energy level of our team? Anything that I do to decrease the energy level of the group is bad.

18. **Outsource.** It's cheaper, faster, and easier. It's not as complicated. You can manage people based on the specific outputs of what you are paying for instead of worrying about all the miscellaneous things you have to worry about with a traditional employee. Less waste. More focus. Having staff wastes so much time unintentionally on stuff that doesn't add value.

19. **Midday Exercise & Socializing.** Going golfing, running, or just grabbing a coffee out of the office with staff is actually a great way to get them to open up. It's also a great way to really connect with them.

20. **Think First.** Some of my comments are far too casual, far too revealing for a business environment. Even swearing. I use swear words too often and they discredit or cheapen me when I use them.

21. **Trust Is Destroyed.** When I talk about people on my team to others on my team, it slowly erodes the trust. I end up leaving those folks to whom I told something in confidence thinking that I likely talk about them behind their backs also.

22. **Nights Are to Recharge.** Don't work nights. Ever. Use them to recharge and relax. Catching up on stuff at night actually slowly burns me out.

23. **Stop Doing & Start Leading**. Or at least if I'm personally doing, have someone from my team sitting with me so they can learn from watching me while I work. I'm more effective when I'm leveraging my time and teaching those on my team how to think also.

24. **Communicate Key Messages Relentlessly**. Only when they are mocking you has it truly sunk it. "Back To The Basics," "The 1-800-GOT-JUNK? Way," "Inspect What You Expect," etc. were all phrases the team members used to tease me about. That meant they got it.

25. **Ensure That Roles Are Clear**. Ensure that the outputs expected have been made clear to everyone. Simple scorecards and reminders about what's important and what's expected will keep people focused on the right things. Clarity of roles will keep people focused on the critically important and highest impact areas vs. just doing busy work.

26. **Define the Right Thing and Show the Path**. Even if this is just sitting in on meetings to ensure that people are clear, purpose and outcomes are focused, and everyone is aligned and working in the same & right direction.

27. **Off-site Meetings Are Valuable**. Every time we took a team off-site for a couple of days there was huge leverage in teambuilding, alignment, communication & focus within the group.

28. **Be Remarkable**. Simply delivering our service isn't enough. We have to be remarkable like the Four Seasons & Seth Godin's *Purple Cow* if we want to stand out and get people talking.

29. **Women—They Talk and Talk**. Women are the core people to wow, influence, network with. They are pre-wired as sneezers. The book *Trends* nailed this concept.

30. **Inspect What You Expect**. As Greig Clark used to say with College Pro Painters, stick your hand in the paint can and see what's really in there. Lift the covers like we did in the call center. Inspect what you expect. Dig into the reports, talk to employees two levels below the director, listen in on calls, etc.

31. **Deadlines**. Build the habit of "doing it" at a specific time in the calendar vs. saying it'll "be done" by a date. Schedule time to do the tasks or projects right into the calendar.

32. **Raise the Bar**. Too many times we hired a person to "do the job" vs. someone who could also add to building the company. Hiring someone who can lead a team that does a certain job is better than hiring someone to just do that job themselves. Sports teams would never hire an average player to "fill" a spot. Hire people to do the job they'll be doing two years out.

33. **Reverse Engineer the Future**. It's just simple backward scheduling applied to everything; like how building a house would be done. Dream. Write down the details of the dream. Figure out the order in which you should do everything, and build off the foundation. Set the plan, milestones, etc., and execute.

34. **Act on Ideas**. Ideas on their own are useless. Sure, you need a simple system to decide what to start when. But too often ideas just keep getting added to a list and don't get started. Lists of random ideas cause more stress for everyone because they make a person feel as if it all has to get done.

35. **Top 5**. Easily one of the most impactful tools if it's used daily. It's the daily focused effort that moves mountains. What are the Top 5 things I need to do today? This simple tool should be used in every company. [Note to readers: Use Teamly, at www.Teamly.com. It will massively help you and your team get more of the right stuff done.]

36. **Stop Doing List**. It's almost as important to be introspective and decide what to stop doing or what to get off your plate as it is to be doing things.

37. **Take Time to Think**. It's when the pen and paper have to come out. It's time away from the office, email, people, time that lets the mind slow down, time when things get clarified and moved forward. Put the laptop away so there are no distractions and no Internet.

38. **Learning**. Apply it to what you are great at vs. trying to get better at weak areas. Apply it to stuff you love doing and around your unique ability areas.

39. **Accept Criticism**. We all have stuff to work on. Accept it when you hear it. Learn from it but don't obsess about it. Everyone has stuff to work on; me included.

40. **Remain Interested, To Remain Interesting**. Friends don't care to hear about my work just like I don't really care about theirs. Surround myself with lots of other interests. Friends and time with them balance me out. Get reignited about my hobbies: golf, tennis, skiing, running, cooking, wine, Burning Man & travel. Thanks to Jillian Dixon Boxer for this life-changing lesson.

41. **Technology**. It is supposed to leverage us and cut costs—not *add* to them. Letting IT infrastructure build up too fast isn't smart. What is smart is using simple things like laptop & software optimization, shortcuts, auto complete, etc. [Note for readers: See chapter 10 for details about what technology to optimize.]

42. **Leverage**. Everything can be leveraged into something else. A lesson for others, a PR angle, a newsletter or blog piece, a starting point for something bigger.

43. **Simon Sinek's Golden Circle**. Why, how, what—inside out. Continue to work from my core purpose. [Note for readers: visit www.StartWithWhy.com for more information on this concept.]

44. **Micromanagement**. Don't major in the minors. If I spent more time creating alignment and developing my team vs. task assignment and follow-up, we could have gotten more of the right stuff done faster. Thanks to my friend Alan Remer for this quote that has nagged me for years.

45. **Make Decisions & Roll Them Out**. People want leaders to make the tough calls, and making tough calls makes leaders.

46. **Look at What's Missing**. Versus focusing on what is there. Finding missing stuff yields quantum leaps.

47. **60 Minute–Proof the Company**. Use the facts, don't exaggerate them, don't overpromise. If *60 Minutes* had to cover it, would it be rock solid?

48. **Cut the Happy Talk**. Everything can be shorter, to the point, clearer. No large presentation folders needed. Don't make me think.

49. **Titles Are Taken VERY Seriously**. Titles like CEO, COO, and VP carry a LOT of weight. Like dropping a boulder into a pond causes ripples, there is a large ripple effect caused by every word or action—

spoken or unspoken—from a person with a big title.

50. CC/BCC: Don't use them—don't copy a person's boss until you talk to the person first. Does the person really need to be copied? BCC destroys trust: i.e., people who use it use it against you, too.

51. 1 Degree of Separation: It will always get back to the other person. Loose lips really do sink ships.

52. Control Emotions: The Transition Curve will happen regardless, but it can be flatter vs. massive ups & downs when you curb negative emotions and overreactions.

53. Rule #6: Don't take yourself so F'n seriously.

54. Cut Deep, Cut Once: If you have to lay off people, do it so that you lay off all the Cs at the same time. (A) You can start rebuilding the culture right away. (B) No one is left gun shy and with survivor's guilt.

55. Nice People Are Nice at ALL Times: If someone is rude to a taxi driver, waiter, etc., that person will be a kiss ass, rude, arrogant, etc., with leadership, customers, and coworkers too.

56. Questions: Ask them more vs. always just saying what I believe. It develops my team more. It also shows them that I really do respect their opinions and ideas and that they are not just my order takers.

57. The 80% Rule for Quick Handoffs: Just get it 80% perfect as fast as possible, and hand it off to someone else who can get the remaining 20% done. It really does work. Use it to leverage my time and skills.

58. EQ: Use emotional intelligence to get all the information before making fast decisions. Slow down on my impulses and show control.

INTERVIEW QUESTIONS

Many of the following interview questions are from surveys, blogs, and lists I've found online over the years. I only listed the ones I really like best, categorized according to personal background, skills and abilities, academic preparation, and other topics.

This list of questions is an excellent resource to use when preparing for interviews with prospective employees.

Problem Solving and Ability to Deal with Adversity

What are your personal goals, and have you achieved them? If not, why?

Who was the most difficult person you've dealt with? How did you respond?

Describe a frustrating experience from work. How did you deal with it?

What are some of the greatest personal challenges you have faced?

How do you handle rejection?

What aspects of your past jobs were most frustrating?

What life experiences have given you the greatest reward?

Can you tell me about the toughest job you've ever had?

What was the most difficult aspect of obtaining a college degree?

Career Goals and Objectives

What are your career interests?

What are your standards of success / goals for a job?

What are your goals and aspirations for the next three years?

What are your long-range goals and how are you preparing to achieve them?

If you could create the perfect job for yourself, what would you do?

Can you tell me about your plans for the future?

What work would you like to do that really interests you?

What is your timetable for achievement of your current career goals?

Relevant Experience

What skills do you possess that will help make you successful in this job?

Why should we hire you?

Have you ever worked in a similar position with another organization, and what did you enjoy most and least about it?

Can you discuss some of your past jobs and what you accomplished in them?

What prior work experiences have you had?

What were your accomplishments in these prior work experiences?

Please tell me about the duties and requirements of your last job.

Elaborate on one of the work experiences listed on your résumé.

What did you enjoy most about your previous job experiences? What did you least enjoy?

In addition to your educational and professional experiences, what else would you like us to know about you in order to make an appropriate decision?

What skills will you bring to the job that will enhance our team or company?

Leadership

What are your major strengths and weaknesses?

What did you see as your major strengths and weaknesses on this job?

What would your last two employers say about you, good and bad?

How would you describe your supervisory/leadership style?

Who or what had the greatest influence on your life?

Can you describe the difference between motivation and inspiration, and how these apply to you in the work environment?

Initiative and Follow-through

What are your greatest achievements at this point in your life?

Tell me about your accomplishments during college that make you proudest.

If friends and colleagues were to describe you to a stranger, what would they say?

What do you consider most important when evaluating yourself?

What were your most significant achievements during this job?

Communication

How would you describe your style of communication?

Tell me about a time you had to sell an idea to someone else.

What do you enjoy doing most?

Tell me about a time you had to present information to a large group of people. How did you feel and how successful were you?

Working Effectively with Others

How well do you work with others?

What are some of the pros and cons of working on a team project?

When have you led a team to achieve a specific goal? What were the results?

What have you admired in people who have previously supervised your work? What haven't you admired in these individuals?

How would you resolve conflict in a group situation?

Creativity and Innovation

What changes would you make in your school's academic program?

Tell me about a time you found a new and better way of doing something.

What was the largest, most creative project you've been involved in to date?

Tell me the most creative solution you have come up with to solve a problem.

Tell me about a time when you had to bring out the creativity in others.

Decision Making

Please tell me about a conflict and how you resolved it.

Tell me about a time you had to make an important decision with limited facts.

Tell me about a time you had to make an unpopular decision.

Tell me about a bad decision you made and what you would have done differently in retrospect.

Delegation and Organization

How do you organize your day?

Tell me about a time you delegated a project effectively.

Describe to me a time when a supervisor delegated a task to you when you had a full workload. How did you handle the situation?

Describe what your closets and garage look like today.

Customer Service and Sales

What personal qualities will you bring to this firm?

Tell me about a time when you dealt with an irate customer.

What does the term "the customer is always right" mean to you?

What's the best example of awesome customer service you've provided?

General

What starting salary do you expect as an employee?

When comparing one company offer to another, what factors will be important to you besides starting salary?

How would you describe yourself?

Name three people who have inspired you and why.

What do you know about our company?

Why are you interviewing with us?

Why do you want to work in the position you are seeking?

What are your expectations of us?

Why did you select us?

GOAL SETTING AND REVIEW PROCESS

PURPOSE

As discussed in chapter 6, Goal Setting and Review (GS&R) is essentially a one-on-one meeting that you have with each person who reports directly to you. The purpose of GS&R is to maintain focus on achieving goals and to provide employees with necessary levels of direction, development, and support.

PREPARATION BY THE EMPLOYEE

To ensure a smooth GS&R with your employees, it's important that each one is ready to give you the numbers for his or her area of the business before the GS&R takes place. It's not unusual for employees to spend fifteen to thirty minutes preparing for this weekly meeting by pulling all the information from the past week together. They should also come with their list of discussion items, concerns, frustrations, questions, ideas, or anything else they want to bring up.

PREPARATION BY THE LEADER

GS&R is almost always the highest-impact event of the week for the leader, and thus excellent preparation is very important. The first step is to analyze the metrics or KPIs for the employee and his or her business areas so you have questions to dig into. How is the employee doing? What red flags do you see in his or her numbers?

Take a step back and ask yourself how the employee is feeling these days. How is his or her commitment level, and how is that commitment level related to each of the key projects he or she is working on or will be working on soon? What "situational leadership" style might you use on various projects you'll be discussing?

Note: A simple GS&R preparation form can be very helpful for both parties.

OPENING HEAD CHECK

Measure the feelings of the employee right off the bat. More than once I've had meetings go exceptionally well by reading the mood of the employee and changing course right away to be more supportive. And often I've missed this step and had these meetings go sideways at a hundred miles an hour. Most likely you'll say something like "So, Bob, how are you doing?" to start the meeting. The next few words he says and how he says them will immediately give you information on his state of mind—*if* you really listen to his response and really care about him as a person.

This skill is especially important to master if you're leading people who work from home or remote offices, in which case you won't be able to read their body language.

If the response to your opening question is favorable, such as "Great" or "Good!" proceed with GS&R. In some cases, though, you might get an unfavorable response such as, "Not so good" or "Brutal." At that moment you have to immediately find out what the problem is and defuse it.

FOLLOWING UP ON THE EMPLOYEE'S GOALS

Following up on the goals is important. As a leader you want your employees to learn to hit the goals they promised to hit. This builds commitment and discipline.

If they hit their goals, praise is due in a big way. If they miss their goals, dig in by asking as many probing questions as you need to in order to uncover the root cause and help move the employee and the project along.

PROBLEM SOLVING

It's part of your job as a leader to develop and refine your employees' problem-solving skills. You're not responsible for solving the problems themselves, but you are responsible for leading and developing a team of people who can solve their own problems.

When an employee misses a goal, ask why. This line of questioning will help generate potential solutions. Help the employee develop a game plan to ensure that future goals are achieved or exceeded.

SETTING SMART GOALS FOR THE NEXT PERIOD

Setting SMART goals is an excellent goal-setting strategy. SMART is an acronym with many variations, but my favorite is this one:

- **S** = Shared
- **M** = Measurable
- **A** = Attainable
- **R** = Relevant
- **T** = Time-based

For a full explanation of each element of SMART goals, see page 28.

HOUSEKEEPING ITEMS

Towards the end of GS&R, you should have a little time left to cover areas that are important to you or your employees. You'll likely also have a list of miscellaneous items to cover.

AGREE ON GOALS SET

Before the meeting ends, ensure that there's complete agreement on what employees plan to get done that week, and be sure that they have the skills and resources to make those goals a reality. Setting up a touch point to check in with the employee mid-week is a good idea.

By the time you end GS&R, you should be able to answer yes to the following questions: Were last week's goals reviewed at the end of the meeting? Were the goals for the next GS&R set? Did the employee receive an appropriate balance of direction, development, and support?

ABOUT THE AUTHOR

For over twenty years, Cameron Herold has been building companies as well as coaching, speaking to, and helping entrepreneurs on five continents as they build theirs. He started BackPocketCOO.com to coach and mentor companies—and help them make their dreams happen. He has twice been the highest-rated speaker at MIT's and Entrepreneurs' Organization's Entrepreneurial Masters Program.

Cameron Herold is one of the country's most innovative business leaders and was a leading force behind one of the most successful new business ventures of the last decade, 1-800-GOT-JUNK?. He was the company's Chief Operating Officer and for nearly seven years, his innovative business leadership helped enable the company to build a presence in forty-six states, nine provinces, and four countries—and to grow from $2 million to $105 million in revenue in six years, with no debt or outside shareholders. 1-800-GOT-JUNK? was also ranked the second-best company to work for in Canada by *Canadian Business* magazine and twice ranked the number-one company to work for in British Columbia by *BC Business* magazine. During his tenure, numerous MBA programs studied the company, including prestigious programs at Queen's University and Harvard.

Prior to this, he was Vice President of Corporate Development at Ubarter.com, a 900-person firm with a $900 million market cap based in Seattle. He was also president of Barter Business Exchange in Vancouver. Previously, Herold served as Vice President of Franchise Development for Coast-to-Coast Franchise Services at Boyd Autobody & Glass.

Overall, he's accumulated twenty years of real-life experience since starting his first real company at age twenty-one. His successes (and yes, the occasional failure) have given him insights into tried-and-true systems that work.

Herold has been an integral part of the sale, branding, and integration of more than 450 franchise locations with three different franchisors. He's worked on the development and deployment of e-commerce and Internet strategies, negotiation of corporate acquisitions, and development of numerous strategic partnerships.

He has a unique understanding of growing companies, having led business areas from operations, marketing, and public relations to strategic alliances, sales, and call centers. His work has helped companies receive press in publications such as the Associated Press, Bloomberg, *USA Today*, the *New York Times*, the *Wall Street Journal*, *Fast Company*, and *Fortune*, as well as TV shows like *The Big Idea with Donny Deutsch*, *The Oprah Winfrey Show*, and *Dr. Phil*.

Cameron gives entrepreneurs the framework and proven solutions that will accelerate revenue, build profitability, and help them avoid costly problems. It really is like having a COO right in your back pocket!